THE INCREDIBLE, WONDERFUL, FLEXIBLE WORLD
OF BUILT-INS

Books by Virginia Frankel

The Incredible, Wonderful, Flexible World of Built-ins
Interior Space, Interior Design
What Your House Tells about You

Rooms designed by Virginia Frankel

A. S. I. D.   Professional Affiliate

Floor plans and sketches executed by Augusto Rojas

THE INCREDIBLE, WONDERFUL, FLEXIBLE WORLD OF BUILT-INS

by Virginia Frankel

A.S.I.D. Professional Affiliate

Charles Scribner's Sons   New York

To the incredible, wonderful,
and very flexible B. V. Wright, Jr.

Copyright © 1977 Virginia Frankel

Library of Congress Cataloging in Publication Data

Frankel, Virginia.
    The incredible, wonderful, flexible world of built-ins.

      1. Built-in furniture   2. Interior decoration.
I. Title.
TT197.5.B8F7   684.1'6   76-51754
ISBN 0-684-14874-9

1 3 5 7 9 11 13 15 17 19 MD/C 20 18 16 14 12 10 8 6 4 2
Printed in the United States of America

CONTENTS

Introduction   ix

1. | General Areas   1

2. | Built-ins That Move with You—   21
     Prefab and Modular Units

3. | Children's Rooms   35

4. | Window Treatments   51

5. | Shelves, Shelves, Shelves   63

6. | Storage   79

7. | The Finishing Touch   105

8. | Multipurpose Rooms   117

9. | Bedrooms and Baths   133

10. | Hobby Centers   153

11. | Do It Yourself   165

12. | Attics and Basements   183

     Credits   195

INTRODUCTION

Building in furniture is not a new concept; furnishings have been incorporated as an integral part of architecture for hundreds of years. The Japanese for many centuries have built ledges in their sparsely furnished rooms and have contributed much to contemporary multilevel design. Their sliding shoji screens for partitioning space and seating arrangements have influenced modern design.

The niche—a recessed wall space—dates back to medieval times. The forerunner of our built-in shelves was used in early Italian and Spanish rooms to hold useful and decorative objects, statuary, religious and otherwise. In the eighteenth century, French and English rooms showed that the niche had grown from being just a decorative object to functioning as storage space, the way it is used today. As architectural styles changed, the shape and design of the niche changed.

As early as the 1500s the English were building bay windows and using them for window seats and storage bins. During the Middle Ages, the trundle bed stored under a larger bed was popular. This piece of furniture, still used today in children's rooms and dens, was important in colonial America. In eighteenth-century France, alcove beds were put into recessed walls and frames built for the niche to save space and reduce drafts. The original Murphy bed was probably invented by French peasants, whose beds were often enclosed in closets with doors or shutters pierced for ventilation—their solution to one-room living and lack of heat. In other countries, too, provincial furniture, especially beds but also cupboards and chests, was largely built in.

In the late eighteenth century and the early part of the nineteenth, the Shakers, a religious sect, built in a great deal of their furnishings. Many of these are still being reproduced, the corner cupboard being one of the most frequently seen.

In royal France there were also *"cabinets particuliers"* or secret rooms for private rendezvous, entered through the backs of wardrobes or through sliding panels in the wall. Unfortunately, today's designers have not come up with a modern version.

Mention should also be made of all the beautiful surface built-ins, such as mantels, cornices, door and window trim, flooring, and, of course, paneling, which is still being widely used today.

Today, built-ins serve aesthetically as well as functionally. Early in this century a new breed of architects began building in again, not only designing functional kitchen and bathroom cabinets, but also adding dropped living rooms for effect, filling niches on each side of fireplaces with bookcases, and utilizing wasted space with other cabinetry. And so the built-in concept flourished.

By mid-century, however, it had been overdone. Racing up and down levels in the living room, falling into conversation pits, meant losing track of the main purpose of furniture—comfort. When we finally abandoned our "Roxy/Music Hall" decor and designed levels that were functional as well as attractive, that fit the needs and life-styles of their users, the built-in really came into its own.

In eighteen years of designing interiors—residences and offices—I have found that there are certain design problems that can be solved only by using built-ins. I see from the design magazines that my colleagues have reached the same conclusion.

It is a misconception that building in is too expensive; built-ins come in all prices. I have proved this many times to my clients' delight, and you will find many examples of inexpensive projects in the following pages.

Built-ins work well in every room in the house. Family rooms and children's rooms are among the best places for total built-ins, since the furniture can also double as storage and play surfaces with minimum maintenance and maximum floor space.

The most valid reason for building in is that you can utilize space that is otherwise a dead loss. In our world of smaller rooms, less storage space, and the necessity of making rooms do double duty, there is an important role for the incredible, wonderful, flexible world of built-ins.

1

General Areas

INTRODUCTION

This book is designed to show you the wide spectrum of ideas for using built-ins in a broad range of rooms, styles, functions, and budgets. It is for the do-it-yourselfer as well as the person shopping for ideas on how to decorate.

While planning the chapters of this book, I found that many categories overlapped, but this only points out the wonderful flexibility of built-ins. They serve many purposes and hide many defects; versatility is their essence. You will be shown examples of designs from basic and conservative to innovative and inventive. This is a wonderful medium for experimenting with a combination of new shapes and/or new materials. The design can be flowing or geometric, combining function with fantasy and comfort with creativity.

The functions of built-ins are many: for books and hi-fi equipment, to store luggage, to display a collection, to serve as a storage-desk unit, to hide tools, or what have you. Properly designed, the same piece can conceal as well as reveal. With built-ins there are all kinds of opportunities for dramatic lighting, color effects, and mixtures. In so many of today's apartments, the builder or architect has left us with unsightly beams, obtruding radiators and air conditioners, badly placed windows, broken-up walls. With judicious planning, these spaces can be better utilized and also given a cosmetic treatment.

There is a variety of unfinished-wood units on the market—bookcases, drawer sections, hutches, desks—which can be designed as a total wall for the built-in look without actually touching the walls. Almost every city has a shop or lumberyard that sells unpainted units. Various standard units are illustrated in this book. The finished modular unit also comes in many designs and finishes, traditional as well as contemporary, available in department or furniture stores, or through your decorator.

Where money is no object, built-ins not only fill a function but can become the focal point of a room. They can be executed in an infinite variety of woods and finishes and combined with other materials—grille doors, marble tops, formica, lined with wallpaper or fabric. In a small room, den, bedroom, breakfast room, or office at home there is a valid reason for combining built-ins with your freestanding furniture. Not only are they marvelous space savers but each section can be planned to hold a specific item or fill a particular need.

So come join us as we explore, explain, and illustrate the incredible, wonderful, flexible world of built-ins.

General Areas

Designed by architect Herbert Kosovitz

Pass-throughs can be used to change living, kitchen, and dining areas. The simplicity of this built-in shelving and storage forms an interesting contrast with the curving iron staircase. Notable features are the exposed lightbulbs, the juxtaposition of circle and square, the mixture of old and new in the furnishings and accessories.

General Areas

3

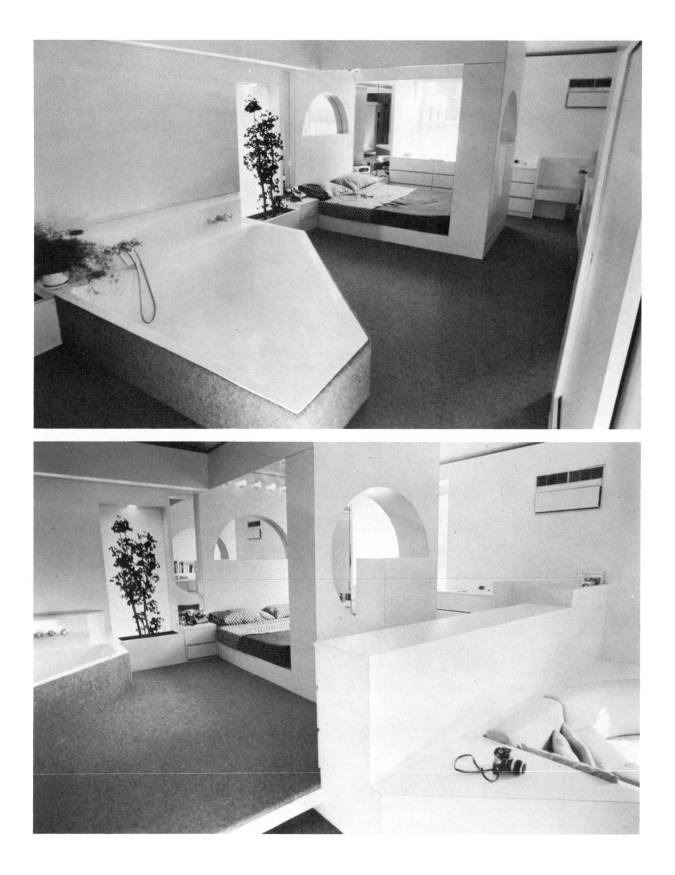

Designed by architect Gamal El-Zoghby

Lots of open space and strong geometric forms make this one room a sculptural environment. Everything is built in, including the lighting. The only decorations are plants. Ample storage space takes care of clutter, and the color scheme is minimal: white, natural wood, and a gray used throughout for the carpeting and upholstery.

General Areas

5

*Antron® nylon carpeting
Photograph courtesy of
Du Pont Company*

A charming extra room can double as a den and guest room. Recessing the bed leaves space for bookcases on each side and cabinet storage underneath.

The fabric lining the bed alcove is also used on the mattress, hassock, and skirted table. Bamboo molding was applied to the cornices, to the doors and walls, and it complements the bamboo side chairs.

This is a simple treatment with a minimum amount of furniture that is easy to reproduce yourself or to have designed for you.

General Areas

6

Designed by architects Robert A. M. Stern and John S. Hagmann

A clean, fresh, uncluttered room, understated and great-looking. The recess formed by the mantel is used for storage below with speakers and niches above. The ledge behind the built-in sofa holds lighting and art objects. All these units seem to flow into one another and fit well into the general architectural scheme.

Designed by Virginia Frankel, A.S.I.D., Professional Affiliate, for Kodel® Fibers, Division of Eastman Kodak

An L-shaped studio apartment with multiple uses. The clients wanted a home not only for their collection of Oriental art but also for their bicycles—the result is a perfect marriage.

Construction started with an L-shaped light box along the window and adjacent wall. This serves as a display ledge as well as a back for the built-in beds. The bicycle storage does double duty as a bar or buffet with a marble top. The beds open to hold the linen, pillows, and blankets.

With beds and buffet counter closed, the room becomes a serene living/dining room with its secrets well hidden.

General Areas

10

Designed by architect Richard Banks

A sculptural home with banquettes and a buffet that sits at the back of the built-in sofa. The floating island at the top of the stairs was planned as an indoor garden and a second sitting room. The furnishings are understated and the eye is always drawn back to the island.

General Areas

11

There are two ways of designing a room. One is planning your furniture first and then working around it. The second way is planning the whole room first and then designing your furniture to conform. This room follows the second plan: built-in light boxes are treated as supergraphics, not only as illumination for the room but as the major unifying design element.

Designed by Reuben de Saavedra, A.S.I.D.

A luxurious office/den designed for an opera buff. The wall adjoining the door was built out to hold a record library. The doors, which are covered with the same leather as the walls, give the impression of a permanent wall when closed.

General Areas

Designed by architects Robert A. M. Stern and John S. Hagmann

General Areas

14

The removal of existing walls and the addition of curved walls in the entrance, living, and dining areas has created a flow from one area to another and also incorporates built-in storage and lighting. This striking buffet wall with flush drawers and recessed lighting is a piece of sculpture in itself. The reverse curve in the hall reinforces the feeling of open space.

Designed by architect William Weber Kirsch
Photograph courtesy of California Redwood Association

A large, central built-in unit is the focal point in the design of this home. The architect, who calls this a transformation rather than a remodeling, turned a compact 1930s house into a wide-open coastal retreat. Interior walls were removed to create an informal, relaxed atmosphere, which characterizes the life-style of the owner. Sleeping and living spaces are indicated rather than designated with sunken areas, cabinets, and bookshelves. Window walls take maximum advantage of an unobstructed view of the California coast.

A platform, accessible from two sides, creates a bed and sitting area, and the extension forms a table. Built-in shelves adjoin the bed space, and the area over the table contains the hi-fi, record player, and record storage. The speakers are placed on top of the column. The third side, abutting the kitchen appliances, is floor-to-ceiling storage.

The mixture of materials—redwood, tile, carpeting, leather, stained glass, and fur pillows—creates an ambience that is architecturally handsome, warm, and livable.

General Areas

15

Designed by Virginia Frankel, A.S.I.D., Professional Affiliate
Photograph courtesy of Allied Chemical
Anso® nylon carpeting

A ski lodge, totally built in, gives maximum entertaining space with the added advantage that the steps are wide enough to accommodate sleeping bags for the extra guests who always drop in.

The steps provide flexible seating and a ledge in back holds decorative objects. The bright, multicolored carpet repeats the colors in the individual wall sections, which are unified by using the carpet-frame color on all wood sections and the chimney. A section of carpet has been cut out and mounted on the wall as decoration.

Designed by architect George Ranalli

The architect-client calls this design a "living machine"; it contains all his basic living needs in a minimum of space. It measures 5 feet wide by 10 feet long; the bed cantilevers over the entrance an additional 2 feet. The "machine" contains a dining space, adjustable bookshelves, storage areas, a bed, and stairs. The entire structure is separate from the existing space, except where it is physically enclosed at the stairs. Combining all these functions into one scupltured unit leaves the rest of the room free and flexible.

General Areas

17

Designed by Stephen Chase of Arthur Elrod Associates, Inc.

General Areas

18

This spectacular playroom in a Honolulu home features bleached rosewood built-in units with recessed lights in each opening to show off a group of Hawaiian artifacts. The recesses are lined alternately with suede and bronze. The bronze soffit has square openings for lighting. The two cabinets frame a mural of ceramic tile, which is also used for the coffee table. The curved corners of the openings, a softening note, repeat the curves of the furnishings.

Designed by architects Robert A. M. Stern and John S. Hagmann

The unbroken sweep of this curved white wall carried out onto the terrace visually enlarges the room and gives the feeling of a super-graphic. The terrace wall, built of sheet metal painted white, contains a storage box for wood. The interior section of the curve and the storage drawers are made of plywood, also painted white. A flush door next to the clock hides a closet where the television set is kept on a wheeled stand to be placed at will.

The stark white curve against the dark wall is all the design that this room needs.

General Areas

2

Built-ins That Move with You— Prefab and Modular Units

INTRODUCTION

The world of movable built-ins ranges from unfinished units to pre-fab walls that are built on casters to whimsical but practical walls of wire rabbit hutches and wooden chicken coops. Bookshelves or cabinets can be free-hung on standards or individual brackets. Sections can be stacked on top of each other or placed side by side.

There are two types of prefab or modular units on the market: unfinished and finished. Unfinished pieces are found in the lumberyard or in cabinet shops and are generally made of pine, birch, or oak, assembled, sanded, and ready for you to install and finish. Only your imagination and your pocketbook limit the choice of finish—paint, paper, foils or fabrics, mirrors and supergraphics, maps and prints covered with a few layers of clear shellac, a collage of favorite photographs, stencils, and appliqués.

There are also many kinds of trim and hardware for unfinished units. Wood moldings come in all widths and styles, metal stripping in all finishes. Handles of metal, wood, enamel, or porcelain can be applied or recessed—or if you wish a sleek contemporary look, touch latches eliminate the need for visible catches.

Top surfaces for desks, buffets, and tables include marble—real or man-made—formica, glass, slate or "colorlith," or inlaid ceramic tiles.

Finished prefab or modular units are available today in a vast selection of materials and styles—all wood or wood finishes, formica, lucite, metal, mirror, lacquers, or combinations of any of these. Modular units are adaptable to every room in the house. Beautifully designed, engineered, and finished, they give the appearance of a built-in wall with the advantage that you can take them with you.

**Built-ins That Move
with You—
Prefab and Modular Units**

Behr International

22

These three photographs show the flexibility of modular units—how a wall can change and grow to fit your needs.

The units are made by Behr International in Germany and distributed in the United States. The basic unit houses drawers, bar, bookshelves, and storage. The addition of three top units creates floor-to-ceiling storage. The unit is extended from wall to wall with the addition of more shelves and two speaker panels.

These units have a lot going for them. They are easily maintained and are available in an unlimited variety of finishes and combinations.

Designed by Carl Fuchs
Photograph courtesy of Window Shade Manufacturers Association

A charming, inexpensive bookcase wall that gives a built-in effect but is easily moved. Wire rabbit hutches have been sprayed white to create this open, unusual unit, which can be adapted to any kind of collection of objects or books.

This unit is an example of the great variety of materials for built-ins or modular units.

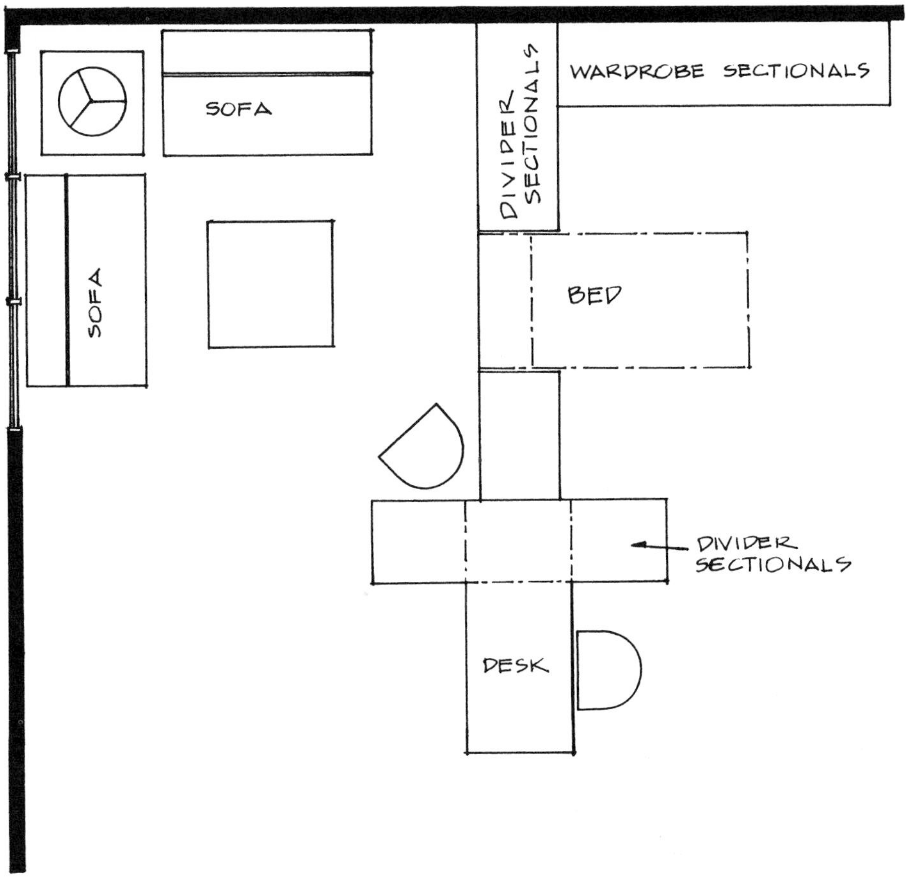
WARDROBE SECTIONALS
SOFA
DIVIDER SECTIONALS
SOFA
BED
DIVIDER SECTIONALS
DESK

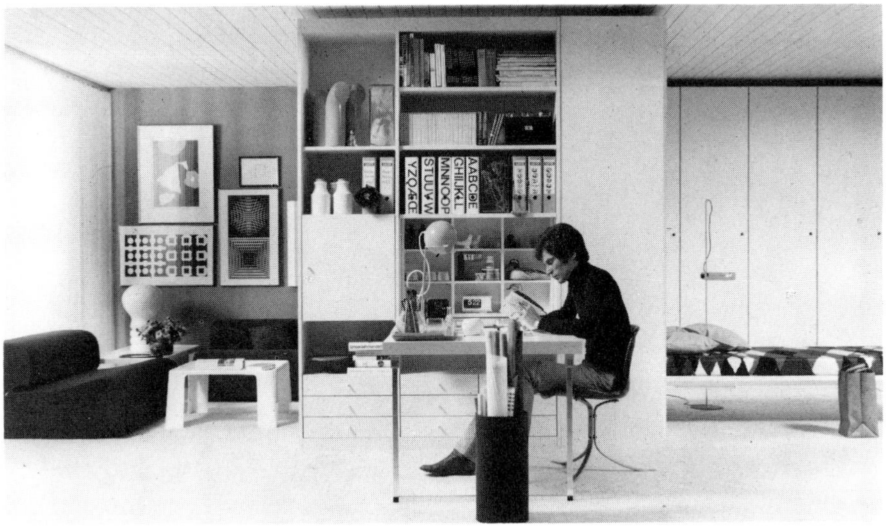

Photograph courtesy of I.C.F.

One multipurpose room for living and working, and it moves with you—that really wraps it up!

A T-shaped furniture plan divides the square room into three areas. The versatile Interlubke system not only provides adequate storage but has a wide assortment of spaces and combinations. Freestanding furniture is kept to a minimum. Sparsely accessorized, the room has a clean, architectural air.

Designed by Albert Herbert, A.S.I.D.

The life and use of modular units can be unlimited. Here the designer has used the Cado System of wall paneling, cabinets, and movable shelves to create an interesting foyer and to give display space for a collection of pre-Columbian art. Mirrored panels between each section give the room extra depth and a sense of greater space.

The sketches show the same units in two other applications which stress the flexibility and movability of a modular system.

Sketch A shows the three units in a living room setting on either side of a fireplace. The paneling is used over the fireplace for continuity, and a rich focal point has been made using existing units.

Sketch B shows the same three units in a guest room/office combination. The units, broken apart around the existing windows, hold the speakers, hi-fi, and television.

**Built-ins That Move
with You—
Prefab and Modular Units**

26

SKETCH A

SKETCH B

. Built-ins That Move
with You—
Prefab and Modular Units

27

The alteration of an old kitchen has resulted in its separation into a small kitchen and dining space through the use of built-in and hanging shelves.

The platform is a 6-inch frame of ¾-inch plywood covered with Amtico flooring. The hanging counter is suspended from the ceiling by ¼-inch steel rods passed through holes drilled in the counter and through the ceiling. The rods are finished with line-grit sandpaper and sprayed with clear spray coating to preserve the finish.

The ceiling beams for the kitchen area form right angles with the beams in the dining area, delineating the space and creating an interesting pattern for a surface that is often neglected. The beams are 1½-inch-wide strips of ¾-inch plywood to which ¼-inch-by-8-inch plywood has been nailed. This forms hollow, lightweight beams that can be made into any length simply by staggering the joints.

The all-white floor, cabinets, furniture, and shelves result in a clean, uncluttered look and provide a wonderful background for plants or any other color accent.

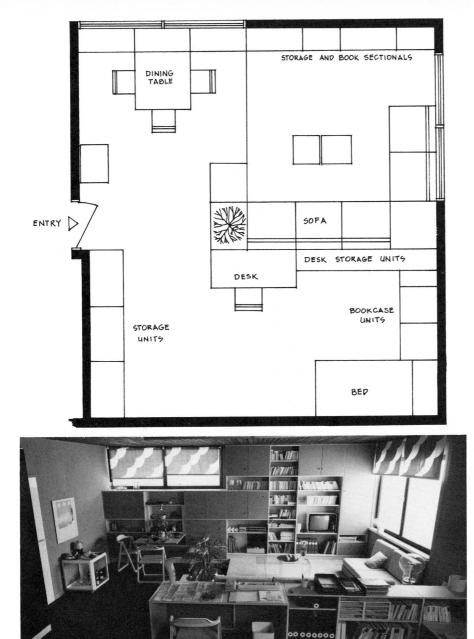

Units by Behr International

Prefabs in a variety of shapes, heights, and depths, in combinations of open and closed units, are used to furnish a functional living and working area. This area can be further divided by hanging matching window shades from the ceiling over the low divider. These prefab units are from Behr International and are available in a wide variety of finishes.

The dining table folds up and the tall units by the door (see floor plan) hold clothing.

This complete living/work space shows how one can not only furnish an interior with built-ins but also conceive, create, and design a total ambience with modular units.

Built-ins That Move with You— Prefab and Modular Units

29

Photograph courtesy of California Redwood Association

**Built-ins That Move
with You—
Prefab and Modular Units**

30

Redwood paneling provides an attractive interior for this teen-ager's room. Built-in shelves and storage are functional, as well as decorative, and with the single platform night table make the best use of a long, narrow room.

Interlubke

The Interlubke system contains various units that can be arranged in myriad combinations. This shows a wall composed of seven units—closets, cabinets, speakers, bar, and drawers—a group that would fit into almost any room in the house.

Built-ins That Move with You— Prefab and Modular Units

31

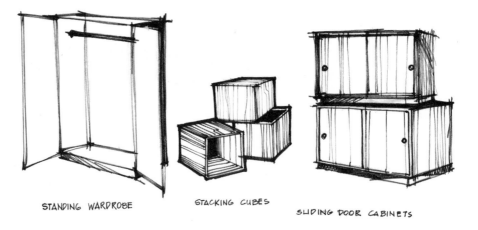

STANDING WARDROBE   STACKING CUBES   SLIDING DOOR CABINETS

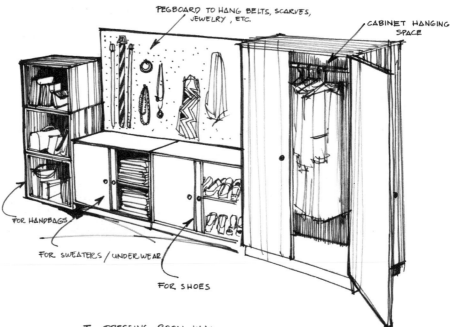

PEGBOARD TO HANG BELTS, SCARVES, JEWELRY, ETC.

CABINET HANGING SPACE

FOR HANDBAGS

FOR SWEATERS / UNDERWEAR

FOR SHOES

I. DRESSING ROOM WALL

I have used the same six unfinished units in three possible groupings to illustrate their flexibility and practicality—they work for the budget-conscious too.

1. *Dressing room wall.* The pegboard hanging over the shoe storage area is decorative as well as functional. Large hooks will hold belts, scarves, and jewelry.

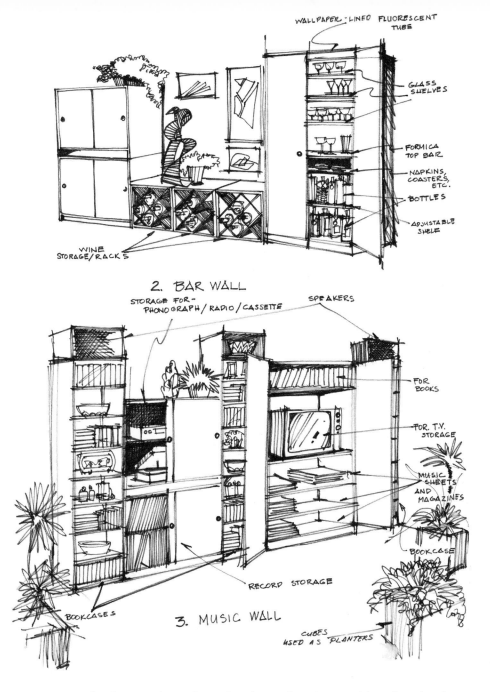

WALLPAPER-LINED FLUORESCENT TUBE

GLASS SHELVES

FORMICA TOP BAR

NAPKINS, COASTERS, ETC.

BOTTLES

ADJUSTABLE SHELF

WINE STORAGE/RACKS

2. BAR WALL

STORAGE FOR PHONOGRAPH/RADIO/CASSETTE

SPEAKERS

FOR BOOKS

FOR T.V. STORAGE

MUSIC SHEETS AND MAGAZINES

BOOKCASE

RECORD STORAGE

BOOKCASES

3. MUSIC WALL

CUBES USED AS PLANTERS

2. *Bar wall.* The standing closet has been fitted out with a formica bar top to resist wetness and stains and a fluorescent light installed with a door switch which goes on automatically. The top shelves are glass, half the depth of the counter to hold glassware. The cubes have been fitted with dividers to hold wine bottles and the mica top creates more counter space for drinks and hors d'oeuvres.

3. *Music wall.* Three units are combined with three custom-made or wall-hung bookshelves to make an entertainment center, holding the television, hi-fi components, records, and speakers. The cubes containing flowerpots and saucers have been painted to match.

These three walls not only have separate uses, but also separate identities, achieved through different finishes, hardware, and accessories.

Built-ins That Move with You— Prefab and Modular Units

33

Photograph courtesy of I.C.F.

This photograph of the Interlubke system shows the effectiveness of combining two finishes, rosewood and formica, in a versatile wall grouping that holds all the at-home entertainment equipment—a television, hi-fi, speakers, and record and tape storage.

3

Children's Rooms

INTRODUCTION

I feel that the best way to design a child's room is to leave as much floor space as possible for play area. The solution? Built-ins, of course—"Child-Proof" or "Early Indestructible"—covered with formica, vinyl wall coverings, hard-surface flooring, and other washable materials. Units can be added or changed as the child grows. Bunk beds can be made into two singles, toy chests converted into foot lockers or storage places, and toy shelves become bookcases. Take advantage of the child's small size to use the upper portion of the room for bunk beds or a play loft.

When designing a room for a young child, where needs and functions will change fairly rapidly, the best solution is often a combination of built-ins or prefabs with some pieces of freestanding furniture that can grow and change with the child. As the child grows older, the need for open floor space decreases. With carefully designed wall built-ins—such as bookcases, chests, and closets with adjustable rods and shelves—a new paint color and/or wallpaper and a change of floor covering can give the room a totally different function and appearance.

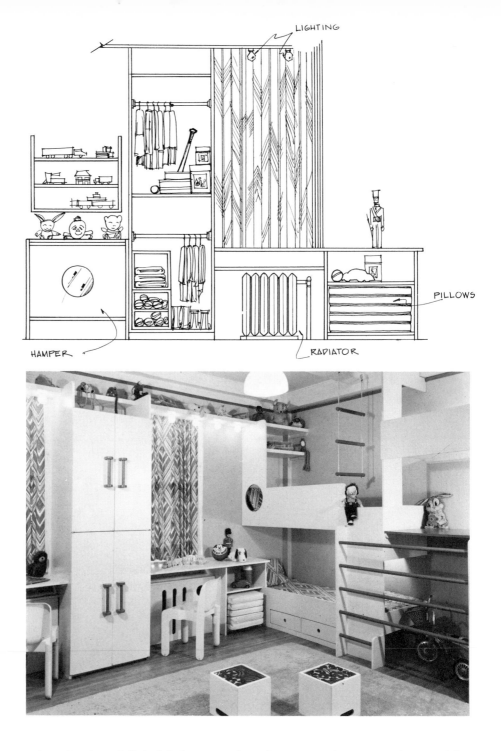

Imaginative, delightful, functional, and creative, this room, designed for two preschool boys, combines all the best features of an environment featuring total use of space, built-in play equipment, and storage.

The bunk beds, play levels, and closet space make the best possible use of the 9-foot ceiling height. All the units are built of U.S. Plywood Duraply panels, ¾-inch ply material coated with a resin fiber that masks the wood grain and provides a smooth surface for painting. The climbing bars and platforms are also painted and covered with two coats of clear scuff-resistant varnish.

Children's Rooms

36

Designed by architect Richard Banks
Photographs courtesy of U.S. Plywood, Duraply Paneling

The lower bunk bed has drawers for storage, and the window wall contains two desks separated by a closet, the lower portion scaled to the children's height and the upper portion for out-of-season storage and special items. The radiators are covered with hinged panels, removable for easy cleaning and repairs (see sketch). The laundry hamper is a part of the total design, with a slot at the top that the children can reach and a hinge at the bottom for removing the soiled wash.

The detailing in this room works for both the children and the adults who have to care for it.

Children's Rooms

37

Designed by Abby Darar for G.A.F. Corp.

Built-ins can be fun as well as functional. In this charming little girl's room in an attic, the designer has constructed a dollhouse in the slope of the eaves and has placed built-in cabinets on each side of the window to create hanging space as well as shelves. A combination desk and dressing table fills the area under the window.

Opposite:

A small child's room designed to allow maximum play space. The built-in bunk beds have a ladder for easy access and a slide for fun.

The conventional window has been replaced by a circular one that opens with a latch and forms a window seat. The cube table and chairs can be built easily, are inexpensive, and can be replaced with other furniture as the child grows.

In designing a small child's room, you can take advantage of vertical as as well as horizontal space by building up, whether for double-layer bunk beds or for play space.

Children's Rooms

38

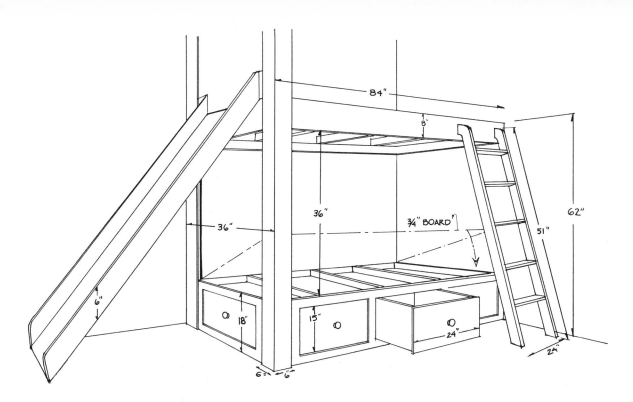

Designed by Virginia Frankel, A.S.I.D., Professional Affiliate

Dividing space seems to make sense in most children's rooms, whether for one or for two—either to divide play and sleeping areas or just to separate areas for children of different ages.

This room is divided by a floor-to-ceiling closet and bookcase to create sleeping and play spaces. The sleeping area is designed on two levels for privacy. The space under the raised bed has a second desk, thus giving each child a separate work area as well.

Children's Rooms

40

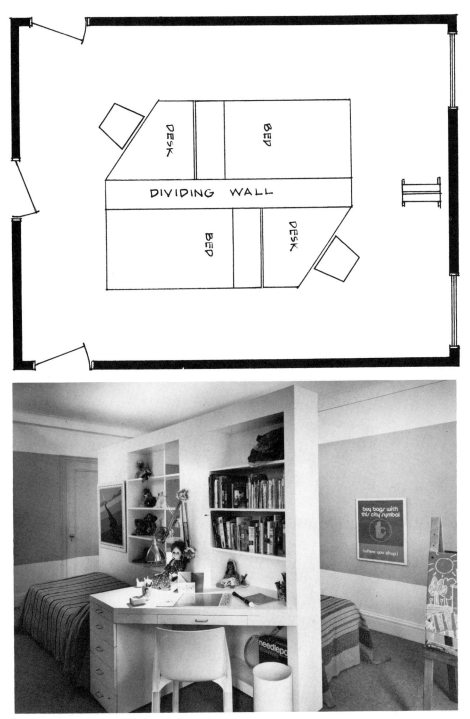

Designed by architects Robert A. M. Stern and John S. Hagmann

A room for two girls with privacy for each—a simple and highly effective use of space. Freestanding built-ins provide each girl with a separate place for sleeping, playing, or working. The shelf and desk unit are reversed on the other side of the divider.

Children's Rooms

41

Designed by François E. Thibeault, A.S.I.D.

An unusual solution for a small space, done with great flair, this wonderfully imaginative boy's room could be developed only by building in. The square room measures 12 feet by 12 feet, so every inch really counts.

The doors were removed from one of the closets and a desk was designed with shelves to fit in. The closet was lined in heavy-textured grass cloth.

The bed is built of 6-inch-by-6-inch beams of natural-colored, sandblasted, and burned wood. It rests on a planked platform, which allows ample room for storing sports equipment. The bedding is strapped around the pillow in bedroll fashion.

Children's Rooms

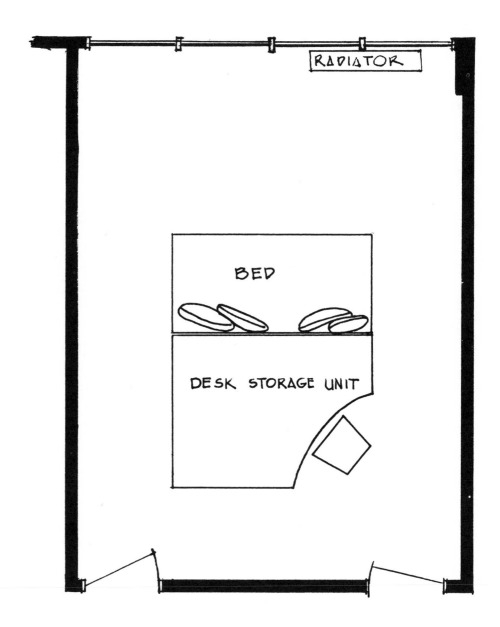

Designed by architects Robert A. M. Stern and John S. Hagmann

A low desk and headboard combination in this young boy's room frees the floor for games, provides storage space for toys and maximum use of the walls for display. The single piece of furniture not only simplifies cleaning and storage but helps give the effect of a much larger area.

Children's Rooms

45

Again a divider and separate levels have been used in a room for two boys. The floating desk/table in front of the window reaches across the room for utility as well as an unbroken look. The 18-inch space taken up by the tables also forms a bookshelf for each side, and the beds make a natural divider.

Designed by Virginia Frankel, A.S.I.D., Professional Affiliate
Anso® carpeting
Photograph courtesy of Allied Chemical Company

A combination of unpainted units and the handyman's skill created this perfect child's room with lots of floor space to play in. The drawer and cabinet units are prefab, fastened together to create steps to the top bunk (or play area). The bunk bed and sleeping platform—6 feet by 36 inches—built to accommodate a sleeping bag, can be put in by the do-it-yourselfer. Bookcases hung on wall brackets store the excess toys and books and the niche under the bed platform creates a private play space.

Children's Rooms

47

Designed by architects Robert A. M. Stern and John S. Hagmann

A child's room that grows with her—the bassinet is replaced by a crib and eventually a bed.

Children's Rooms

48

The drawers, closets, and open shelves will change as the child's needs change. The shelves holding toys will contain books, record player, and bibelots. A perfect example of how less can be more.

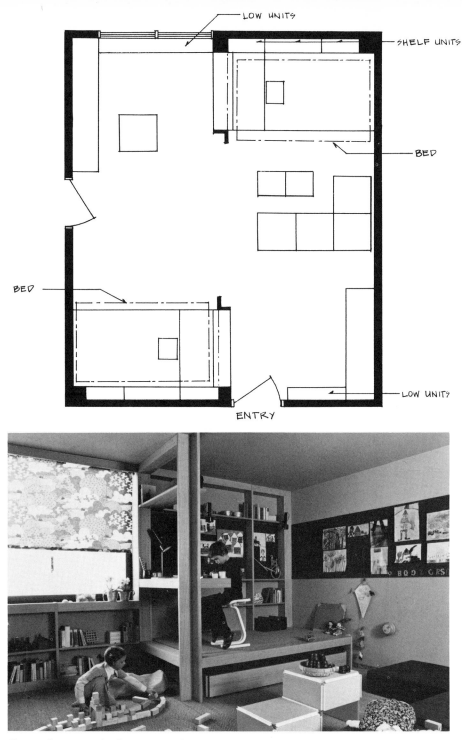

LOW UNITS

SHELF UNITS

BED

BED

LOW UNITS

ENTRY

Photograph courtesy of Behr International

Modular posts, shelves, and wall units can divide work, play, and sleeping space in one room for two children.

The post modulars form a raised work space with a trundle bed underneath. The low units hold toys and books and the floor-to-ceiling ones have drawers and closet space.

Keeping the units around the perimeter of the room frees the center for play space.

Children's Rooms

49

4

Window Treatments

INTRODUCTION

Window walls offer unlimited possibilities for building in, whether for function, a decorative lift, or both.

Window walls often present many architectural problems all at once, such as the radiator and air conditioner, a miscellaneous collection of beams, and off-center or badly placed windows. Sometimes these can be covered by floor-to-ceiling draperies, but these, unfortunately, cut out the light and when opened reveal all the uglies.

Windows can be a natural display area, for plants, a glass collection, sculpture, shells, or whatever, by placing glass shelves against stationary panes. Or, they can be framed with shelves or closed cabinets for hi-fi or speaker storage. Look carefully at your windows and you will see waste space that can be saved.

Window space, which is often a problem, with careful planning can become a decorative plus. The windows are left free for individual treatments, with shades, shutters, beads, or draperies that control light.

Off-center windows can be camouflaged by combining your window treatment with shelves, and the space above and below the window—often an awkward blank—can be filled in. For city dwellers, for whom soot and dirt are often the main concern, a washable blind or shade framed with shelves is a perfect answer. In children's rooms, where space is needed for toys and games, shelves provide easy access below the windows and space for "no-touch" fragile dolls or toys on top until the children are old enough to play with them.

The kitchen is another room where curtains are not advisable, because of the grease from cooking. Glass shelves in these windows can be filled with pots of herbs or with decorative objects.

Windows should be both functional and decorative and should be thought of not only as a source of light but also as part of the overall wall design.

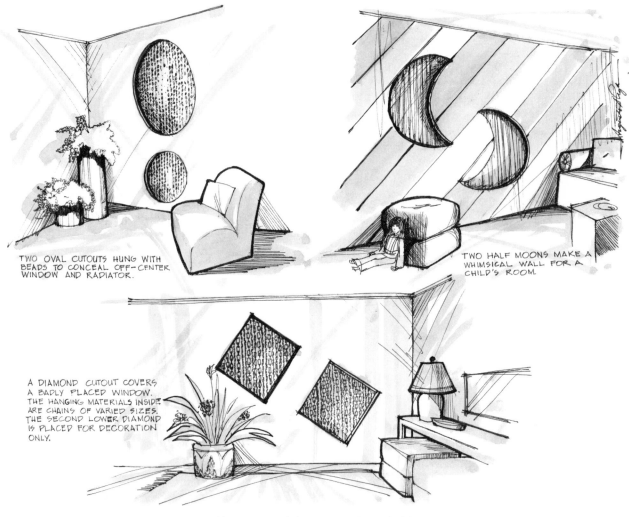

TWO OVAL CUTOUTS HUNG WITH BEADS TO CONCEAL OFF-CENTER WINDOW AND RADIATOR.

TWO HALF MOONS MAKE A WHIMSICAL WALL FOR A CHILD'S ROOM.

A DIAMOND CUTOUT COVERS A BADLY PLACED WINDOW. THE HANGING MATERIALS INSIDE ARE CHAINS OF VARIED SIZES. THE SECOND LOWER DIAMOND IS PLACED FOR DECORATION ONLY.

Designed by Virginia Frankel, A.S.I.D., Professional Affiliate

Window Treatments

52

Plywood paneling as a freestanding wall can do magic to hide or alter a bad window. Whether your window is off center, badly placed, too high, or an odd shape, this is your solution. Fasten the plywood to the floor and ceiling with angle irons to keep it stable. The covering is up to you. A false wall can also cover floor radiators and a window air conditioner, but I suggest using beads, rows of chains, or open-weave casement cloth to allow the air to pass through.

Designed by Emily Malino, A.S.I.D.
Photographs courtesy Window Shade Manufacturers Association

This interesting and functional window wall has been built to form storage space for a collection of Japanese lacquer. The cabinets take only 12 inches from the floor space and fluorescent lighting is concealed behind the cornices over the cabinets and windows. The shades are white shantung decorated with black tape and are framed by slim shutter screens.

Drama and practicality are combined in this arrangement. The simplicity of the room is further enhanced by the black-and-white color scheme.

Window Treatments

Room designed by Virginia Frankel, A.S.I.D., Professional Affiliate
Photograph courtesy of Window Shade Manufacturers Association

This room has been pictured many times but still is one of my favorites. It illustrates that careful use of space and a combination of bright colors with a mixture of textures can make a window wall the focal point of a room, even though hampered by an ugly, old-fashioned radiator and an air conditioner.

Bookshelves are built around, over, and under the windows. The vertical shades are in varying colors—pinks, greens, magenta, and white. They were selected not only for their look but for the versatility of light control they allow. The strong contrast of vertical and horizontal lines side by side forms a striking design accent.

The green color inside the bookshelves is picked up from one of the shade cloth colors.

The oak parc de Versailles coffee table is accented by the white flokati rug and the corner mattress-covered banquettes double as sofas and guest beds.

Window Treatments

Designed by Reuben de Saavedra, A.S.I.D.

This sophisticated window treatment covers an off-center window and provides more storage space. A false wall 12 inches from the window wall allows for shelf storage behind the horizontal metal louvers.

Beams are lowered from the ceiling, to create architectural interest and also to house the recessed lighting. Fluorescent strips are placed behind each louvered section to give equal light and further the illusion of three windows instead of one.

The white upholstery and carpeting contrast dramatically with the tortoise vinyl wall coverings.

The built-in shelf behind the sofa is unobtrusive, to highlight the owner's collection of prints and drawings.

See the plan on page 56.

Window Treatments

55

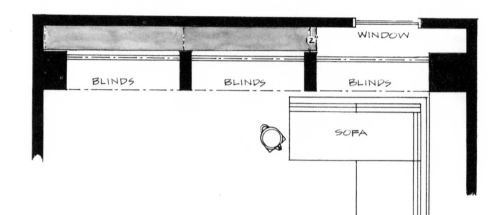

STORAGE SPACE

Opposite:

These before and after photographs show the dramatic differences that built-ins made in this semibasement catchall by turning it into a sophisticated den/library. The walls were paneled in U.S. Plywood and the space on each side of the windows was filled with bookcases connected by a window cornice. The draperies were hung floor to ceiling to make the ceiling appear higher.

The other side of the room has built-in, lighted, slanted display areas to show art books or prints and extra-large cabinets below for art book storage.

Window Treatments

56

Window Treatments

Designed by Virginia Frankel, A.S.I.D., Professional Affiliate
Photographs courtesy of U.S. Plywood/Champion International

57

Window walls lend themselves to the addition of closets, shelves, or storage. This window has been flanked by two closets to form a sewing center. The cabinet on the right holds the dressmaker's dummy and the portable machine. The parsons table at right, angled to the window, becomes a desk when cleaned off, and the shelf space at each side of the window is recessed to hold books and office supplies.

The sketch shows another version of this window treatment, to make a dressing table for a bedroom.

Window Treatments

59

ELECTRICAL FIXTURE

STRIP FOR SLIDING DOORS

The door to the terrace plus off-center windows, radiator, and beams made this wall an architectural horror. The only way to improve it was by total cover. The shoji screens were built on a track for easy access to the door, heat, and air conditioner, and they were filled with an open-weave casement to let light in but hide the irregularities (shown in the sketch).

A row of fluorescent lighting was installed behind the top fascia to carry out the backlighted effect at night. The corner beam was negated by built-in bookcases, which run the length of the wall.

Window Treatments

60

Designed by Virginia Frankel, A.S.I.D., Professional Affiliate
Carpeting courtesy of Enka Mills

An all-white-and-yellow color scheme makes this a pleasant and sunny room in which to work. The skirted table hides a file cabinet and the fabric-covered boxes on the top shelf hold photographs and papers.

In designing this room as my office, den, and guest bedroom, I had to make every inch count and yet keep an uncluttered feeling.

Window Treatments

Designed by Virginia Frankel, A.S.I.D., Professional Affiliate

A window wall full of goodies: radiator and air conditioner, unmatched beams, and to really top it off, an off-center and no-view window! A wood Mondrian-type construction separates the areas, including the space on the left, which is used for storage. Four different-colored window shades were hung to form a shade abstract and to conceal everything behind. An added touch was placing fluorescent tubes behind the large shade to silhouette the sculpture and plants.

5

Shelves, Shelves, Shelves

INTRODUCTION

Bookcase walls are probably one of the first designs that occur to people when they think of built-ins. There are endless combinations, uses, and styles for them. Many other components can be incorporated—a wall desk, bar, drop-down dining table, Murphy bed, lighted niches for sculpture or paintings, and hi-fi components. The bookcase wall can be freestanding and used as a room divider or screen. Units can be divided and placed around a room in different sections or around doors, windows, or waste space created by beams or fireplace walls. Simple pine shelving can be used and edged with carved pilasters and cornices. If you are in a rented apartment or home, marking the sections in 18-, 24-, or 36-inch pieces with a back will make moving easier. The same measurements apply to working with modular units. If you do not plan to move, or if cost is a factor, they can be attached directly to the wall. In most units, adjustable shelves are advisable, with one permanent shelf in the center for additional support.

There are unlimited decorative finishes. The shelves can be painted one color and the interior a contrasting color, or the interior colors can be varied in a single unit, giving a Mondrian effect to the entire wall. Wallpaper can be effective when the scale and pattern are correct. Marbleized papers, stripes, and small all-over patterns are possibilities. Natural wood, either oiled or varnished, can give a rich look to a library, den, or period room. Edging the shelves with metal stripping, such as copper or aluminum, will provide a contemporary custom look to your shelves. A mirror placed on the back of the shelves reflects a collection and visually increases the size of a room.

If your wall space is limited or broken up, free-floating shelves can solve your problem and form a pattern by themselves with irregular sizes and varied placement.

There is not a room in the home where shelves cannot be used, and there are systems that will fit into any room or decorative scheme.

Freestanding shelves line this wall. A freestanding pillar built to ceiling height can, as does this one, fill many functions.

Place the pillar 42 inches from the wall; the shelves can be as wide and deep as you require. Here the pillar is sketched as a square, but it would be equally effective as a rectangle.

The desk side becomes a brace to hold the table top with brackets, and the opposite side is a small service bar. The other sides have shallow shelves to hold paintings and a collection of miniature objects.

Shelves, Shelves, Shelves

64

Designed by Virginia Frankel, A.S.I.D., Professional Affiliate

Pine shelves were painted white to match the woodwork in this room, and the back is painted in the same bright yellow as the walls. The color contrast and the irregular placement of shelves lend interest to a simple installation.

Adjustable shelves are useful for change of placement, and the single shelf along the top pulls the unit together and provides storage for speakers, record boxes, and other objects.

The two problems to be overcome on this wall were a door at one corner and one heavy beam at the window wall. By angling the first unit from beam depth to the side of the door, the wall is given an unbroken appearance.

Shelves, Shelves, Shelves

65

Designed by Stephen Chase of Arthur Elrod Associates, Inc.

Shelves, Shelves, Shelves

66

The designer of this striking office/den in a Florida condominium has used a group of different-size lighted niches to show off a collection of porcelain and shells. The niche over the desk hides a television set, which can be concealed with a wooden sliding door (the photograph shows it closed). The textured and notched wood easily conceals storage areas at the breaks of the paneling.

Designed by Virginia Frankel, A.S.I.D., Professional Affiliate

These bookshelves were designed for a collector of art books. The center slanting shelf, constructed to hold the volumes open for a changing display, and built-in lighting make this area the highlight of the wall. The bottom cabinets are oversized to hold large volumes; vertical slots in the cabinets keep the books and covered paper folios from buckling.

The sketch shows how the slanting shelf could be incorporated into a den wall to hold an atlas or dictionary for easy viewing.

Shelves, Shelves, Shelves

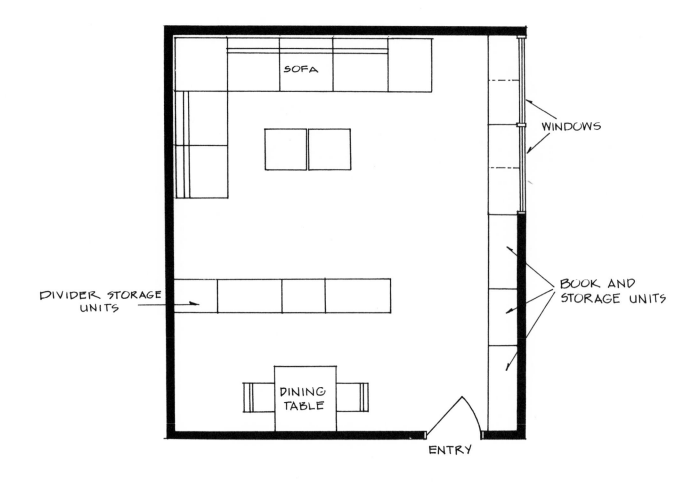

A large space divided by a floor-to-ceiling combination of bookshelves, bar, cabinets, and vitrine units manufactured by Behr International (see floor plan). The back is finished to form the wall of the dining area.

The space under the windows has been used for additional bookshelves, showing that the units do not always have to meet the existing structure: plants and accessories camouflage the fact that the tops of the bookcases do not meet the windowsill. In one photograph, the bar and refrigerator unit are shown open.

This combination of shelves and cabinets provides ample storage as well as niches and display spaces. This center divider can be turned either to the library or to the dining side.

Shelves, Shelves, Shelves

Shelves, Shelves, Shelves

Behr International

Designed by Noel Jeffrey

Home offices can be as intricate or as simple as desired. These photographs show an office corner incorporated into a living room and a separate office unit.

Posts holding glass bookshelves, recessed lighting, and a plant trough give a strong geometrical pattern to the corner of this room. Do-it-yourselfers can use these shelves in a variety of patterns.

The second room is an office shell, a symmetrical arrangement of shelves, desk, and paneling. Rounded corners give added interest. File cabinets have been incorporated in the base of the back unit. Recessed lighting completes the clean architectural feeling of the room.

Shelves, Shelves, Shelves

71

Designed by Augusto Rojas

Free-floating shelves are among the most flexible of all the prefab units. They can be butted together to form a long shelf or staggered for a fresh and more casual look, as in this room. The permanent top cornice hides lights to illuminate the ceramics collection.

As the sketch shows, in an informal country dining room where space is at a premium, these shelves could hold dinnerware for easy access.

Shelves, Shelves, Shelves

72

Designed by John Elmo, F.A.S.I.D.

Designed by Edmund Motyka, A.S.I.D.

Shelves, Shelves, Shelves

74

A marvelous book wall including a never-used window forms a pleasant contrast to the dark walls and a display area for plants and objects. These strips and brackets are inexpensive and easy to install, and they do double duty as bookends. On the right, they have been worked around two unfinished cabinets, stained to match the shelves.

Designed by Edmund Motyka, A.S.I.D.

Book walls, record storage, and enclosed speakers. The cabinets hold the record player and hi-fi equipment. The wall paneling and the recessed bed area impart a warm look to this small room.

A decorative, permanent book wall was built to incorporate two open spaces, one for a chess table and chairs and the other for an armchair to complete the seating area with the sofa.

The bookcases reach the ceiling to give the illusion of greater height and to turn the beams into a decorative plus. The built-in light units not only highlight the art but form a pleasant pattern on the wall.

Shelves, Shelves, Shelves

76

Designed by Virginia Frankel, A.S.I.D., Professional Affiliate

Designed by Reuben de Saavedra, A.S.I.D.

Another type of shelf unit, lucite with fluorescent tubes built in for accents, is particularly striking as shown here against a dark wall. The openings are designed to hold the speakers, a television set, and record player. It is built in two sections, which not only enables you to move it around in your apartment but also makes it easier to move it into your dwelling by elevator and/or through a narrow hallway.

This brings up a subject that we have not yet dealt with: premeasuring. If you live in an apartment building, find out the height of the freight elevator. If the door to your room angles off a narrow hall, make sure the piece is not too long to go around the door jamb. I have heard of people ordering a 10-foot sofa and not being able to get it into the apartment. If you do not know what size it should be to enter a particular space, your moving man or designer will be able to tell you.

Shelves, Shelves, Shelves

6

Storage

INTRODUCTION

You can never have enough storage. Built-ins are the perfect places for storage, in well-designed, functional units.

First, list the items you need to store and their measurements. Then choose the room or closet in which you want to keep them and design around the objects. Keep in mind how often you use these things. Those used frequently should be in the center for easy access; the least used, such as luggage, out-of-season clothes, or dead storage, should be placed at the top. The bottom space is useful for bulky item, such as blankets.

Storage units can also be incorporated into book walls, set under bunk beds, or used to fill in a small wall or odd corner in a room.

Shown in this chapter are custom-built storage units as well as prefab units that have been chosen for their practicality and ease of installation. You will notice that custom units are shown only in areas that cannot be filled by ready-mades. If you are going to buy storage units, take your list of items and measurements with you when you shop to get the maximum use from your furnishings.

Designed by architects Robert A. M. Stern and John S. Hagmann

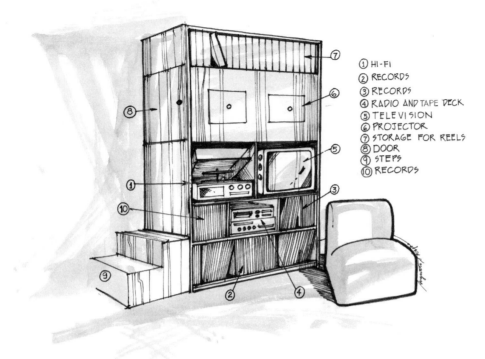

1. HI-FI
2. RECORDS
3. RECORDS
4. RADIO AND TAPE DECK
5. TELEVISION
6. PROJECTOR
7. STORAGE FOR REELS
8. DOOR
9. STEPS
10. RECORDS

Designed by Virginia Frankel, A.S.I.D., Professional Affiliate

Opposite:

With a minimum of furniture and a judicious use of built-ins, this has become a compact living and entertaining apartment. Large-scale cabinet work covers two walls of the living room, providing space for books, a speaker system, a mirrored bar, and ample storage.

The small foyer is made to appear larger with the formica shelf on adjoining walls, and the two horizontals make the ceiling appear higher—an effective contrast for the dark walls.

Without the custom design of building in, this space would not be as effectively and efficiently used.

Above:

This self-contained entertainment center holds a projector with storage for reels and tapes as well as a television set, radio, tape deck, hi-fi, and records. The small panel on the top opens when the projector is in use; a small fan keeps the cabinet from overheating.

The speakers were not incorporated into the unit but could be placed at each side of the wall.

Storage

81

Behr International

Storage units convert this large room into separate dining and living spaces. The center L-shaped divider is low, to give an illusion of more space; it holds additional storage and bar equipment.

The closeup shows the sliding tray drawers used for linens. The shallow drawer on the right accommodates silverware, placemats, and other small accessories. Other tableware is kept in the units on the living room side, a necessity when kitchen storage is limited.

These prefab units from Behr International have the advantage of being able to be rearranged at will.

Storage

82

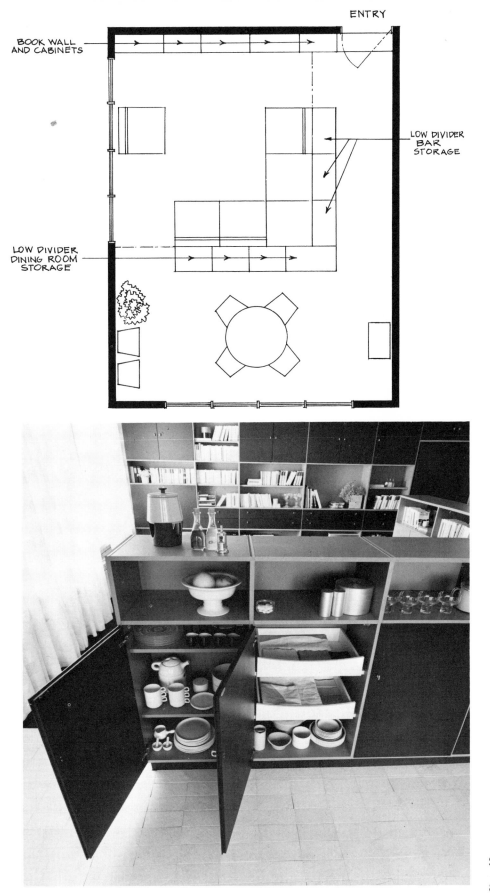

Storage

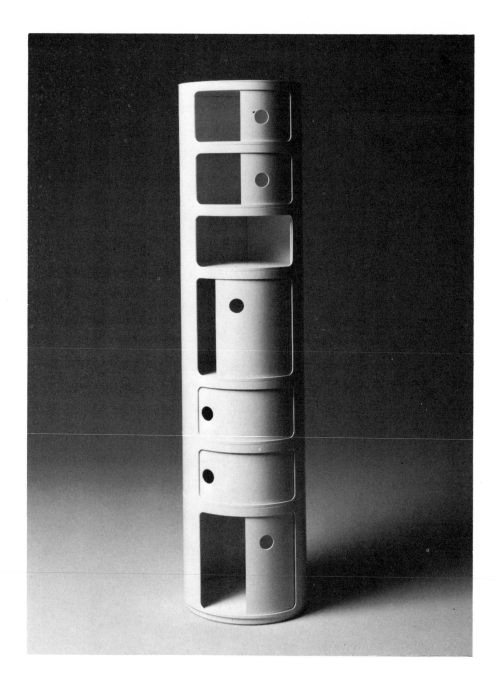

Beylerian's stacking units can be lined against a wall in varying heights to form exciting and unusual storage walls. They would be effective in any room in the house. They are shown here in a den/study where there is a multitude of small items to keep hidden.

Designed by Virginia Frankel, A.S.I.D., Professional Affiliate

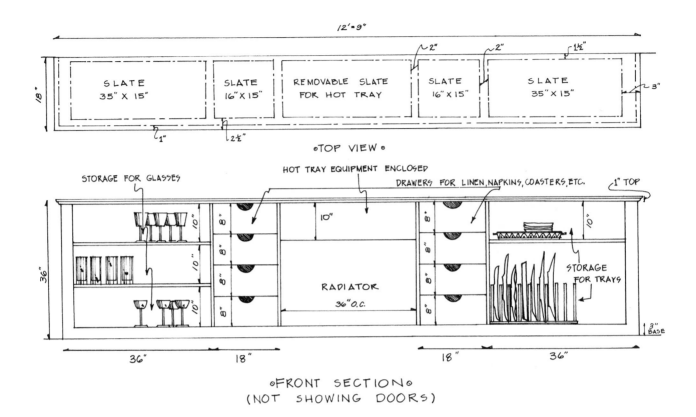

12'-9"

18"

SLATE
35" X 15"

SLATE
16" X 15"

REMOVABLE SLATE
FOR HOT TRAY

2"

SLATE
16" X 15"

2"

1½"

SLATE
35" X 15"

3"

1"

2½"

∘ TOP VIEW ∘

STORAGE FOR GLASSES

HOT TRAY EQUIPMENT ENCLOSED

DRAWERS FOR LINEN, NAPKINS, COASTERS, ETC.

1" TOP

10"

10"

10"

10"

8"

8"

8"

8"

10"

8"

8"

8"

8"

10"

RADIATOR

36" O.C.

STORAGE
FOR TRAYS

36"

3"
BASE

36"

18"

18"

36"

∘ FRONT SECTION ∘
(NOT SHOWING DOORS)

This classic example of the built-in is both aesthetically pleasing and functional, and it seems to be an integral part of the architecture. It serves not only as a radiator cover but also as a 16-foot buffet surface and storage area and has a built-in hot plate with a removable slate cover.

The wood for the cabinets was perfectly matched to the paneling and the top was covered with slate to withstand water stains and heat. One section has partitions for tray storage, another for glasses, and a third has drawers for napkins and table mats. The radiator section has grille doors that open for easy access. This wall is curved; but the sketch shows a straight wall with similar 18-inch modular units.

Storage

86

Designed by Virginia Frankel, A.S.I.D., Professional Affiliate

Storage

87

Designed by architects Robert A. M. Stern and John S. Hagmann

An apartment in one of New York's older buildings was extensively remodeled by enlarging and regrouping living and dining areas around a spatial drum in which is housed a guest bath, music center, sideboard, and bar. Ceilings were lowered to provide lighting for an art collection; the new dining room ceiling is octagonal.

The sideboard on the exterior of the central drum has niches for art objects, a large, sweeping surface for a buffet, and flush drawers for storage.

A striking combination incorporating utilization of space and total design.

Photo courtesy of the Maytag Company

If you are remodeling or rebuilding your kitchen, you have the luxury of incorporating your own ideas into the design.

In this plan for a kitchen wall the washer and dryer have been recessed and cabinets put above to hold laundry needs. The oven is recessed into the wall and the narrow drawers below hold rolls of kitchen wrap and kitchen hardware. The cabinets above are for items not used frequently. The desk makes menu planning and writing up marketing lists more comfortable.

DESIGN A

Designed by Virginia Frankel, A.S.I.D., Professional Affiliate

Boxes for storage: a multitude of uses and combinations and various sizes and shapes to suit your needs.

Design A shows three boxes nailed together and wall-hung to make a bar. The bottom box has been partitioned for wine storage and the two side ones hold glasses or bottles. A glass shelf placed across the three boxes gives extra surface space and makes a small storage area for napkins, coasters, or whatever.

Design B shows the same three boxes used as a stereo center. These, too, are wall-hung, and the bottom two are hung "on point" to create an additional design element. The top box holds the phonograph, and the radio and tape deck are placed on top. The two "on-point" boxes hold records, and the V space between them has ample storage for tapes.

Design C shows the three boxes wall-hung and placed in a step formation. The top and bottom boxes have a hidden hinged door with a touch-latch opening to keep the front surface flat. The center box has been left empty to hold potted plants for a design accent.

DESIGN B

DESIGN C

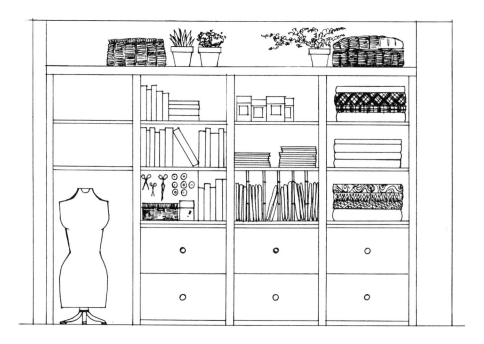

Measuring and planning for storage are discussed in the introduction to this chapter. Following these guidelines, this sewing wall was designed to hold fabrics, patterns, and the dummy. The section next to the sewing table has a slanted shelf to hold spools, scissors, and thimbles and space into which to slide the sewing machine when it is not in use. The storage area is hidden by hand-painted window shades, which are not only decorative but functional.

Photograph courtesy of Window Shade Manufacturers Association

Storage

93

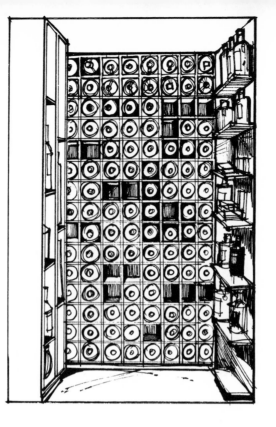

WINE CLOSET

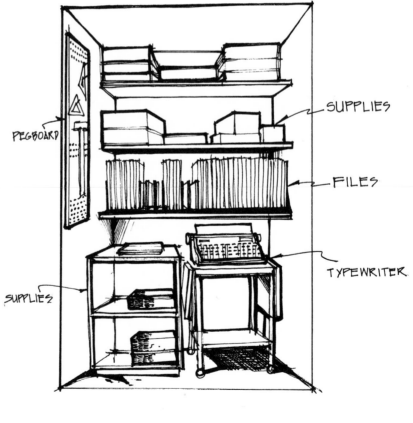

PEGBOARD

SUPPLIES

FILES

SUPPLIES

TYPEWRITER

Storage

94

OFFICE CLOSET

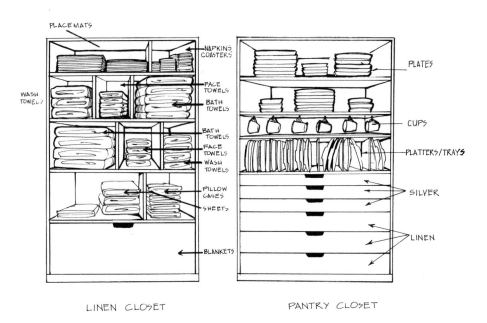

PLACEMATS

NAPKINS
COASTERS

WASH
TOWELS

FACE
TOWELS

BATH
TOWELS

BATH
TOWELS

FACE
TOWELS

WASH
TOWELS

PILLOW
CASES

SHEETS

BLANKETS

PLATES

CUPS

PLATTERS/TRAYS

SILVER

LINEN

LINEN CLOSET   PANTRY CLOSET

Designed by Virginia Frankel, A.S.I.D., Professional Affiliate

Here an average 42-inch closet has been partitioned into many closets. Space is broken up for special items—washcloths, silverware, hats, a typewriter—to keep everything neater and make it easier for you to find what you need. For instance, in the linen closet, you can break up the shelves and storage for each bath item. If you have different-size bed linens, store these on separate shelves. It is helpful if you mark your shelves with labels. The same should be done for dress bags, shoe boxes, and any storage items that are hidden in boxes such as stationery supplies.

In the wine closet, label the shelves to show name and year. Every inch can work for you if carefully thought out.

Pegboard on the inside of the door is helpful for small objects—belts, scarves, and so on. In your office closet, small baskets can hold pencils, rulers, and an inventory of supplies.

To support heavy items (blankets, stationery, etc.) 3/4-inch lumber is recommended for shelves. In vertical partitioning, 1/4-inch or 1/2-inch shelving is sufficient. The interior of your closet can be treated with mirrors (effective for a wine closet), wallpaper, or paint.

Storage

95

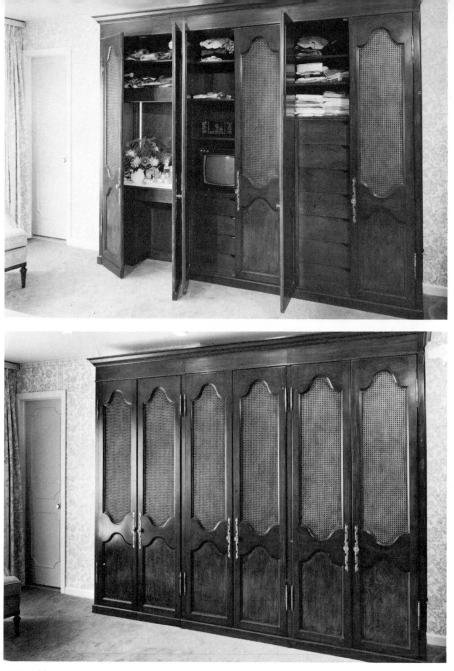

Designed by Virginia Frankel, A.S.I.D., Professional Affiliate

One wall—many uses. The armoire was designed and built in three sections of 36 inches each for ease in moving and flexibility to allow placement in different settings. The crown is in one piece to give the appearance of a single unit. If the units are separated, a new crown or crowns would have to be made.

The left-hand section holds a dressing table with recessed top lighting and a carara glass top and small drawers for cosmetics, and the top shelves hold scarves, gloves, and so on. The center unit (unisex) has the television, drawers, and shelves. The right-hand section is a chifforobe for the man of the house.

This is one piece of furniture that takes the place of four.

Storage

SCULPTURED BUILT-INS

As this book developed, I felt myself surrounded by rectangles and squares and weighted down by straight lines. But built-ins can be sculptured—fun and functional all at once. With that in mind, I designed this group.

Geometrics lend themselves to a variety of patterns and uses. The sizes and interiors can vary depending on need. They can hold shelves, drawers, bar units, and lighted mirror sections in keeping with the room and function. The cabinets can be built on the wall or separately and then wall-hung in a variety of positions. Stainless steel, in brushed or polished finish, placed on a dramatically colored wall would be striking. They also lend themselves to wood, formica, or plastic.

This collection, designed by Virginia Frankel, will be on the market in the fall of 1977.

Designed by Virginia Frankel, A.S.I.D., Professional Affiliate

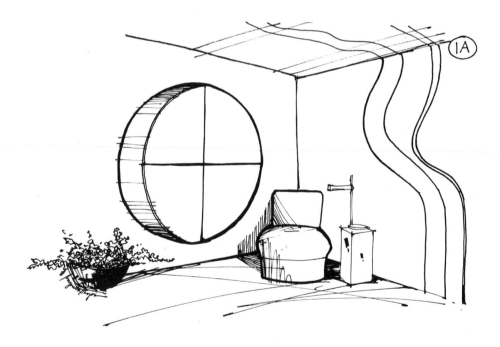

Storage

98

Design 1 shows two half-round cabinets placed in different positions for design and function; 1A shows the two halves placed together.

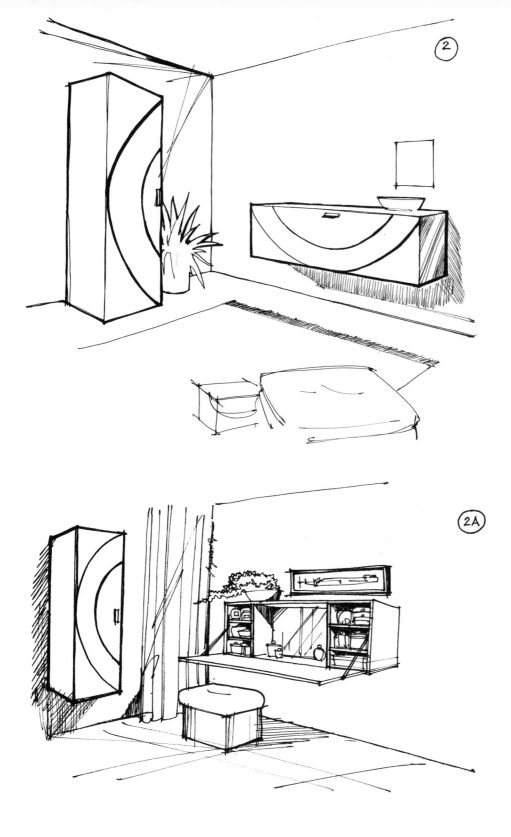

Design 2 shows horizontal and vertical cabinets with colored formica inlays. These would be especially good in a bedroom, the horizontal forming a dressing table and the vertical either holding drawers or providing space for hanging dresses. In 2A the horizontal one is open.

Storage

Design 3 shows three triangles placed together and at different angles. 3A shows them hung as verticals; 3B, as horizontals; 3C and 3D show other variations.

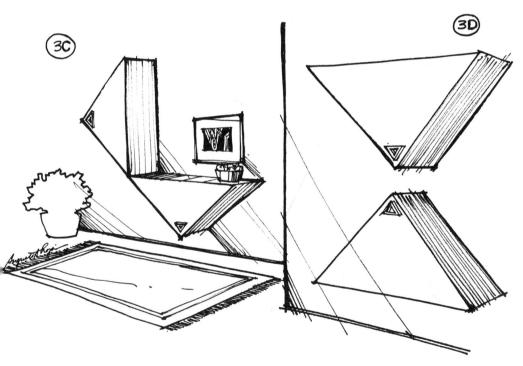

Storage

102

Design 4 shows a series of triangles—a striking buffet-foyer unit. 4A is a different arrangement of the same triangles.

Design 5 shows two sizes of rectangular cabinets. On the following page we show them arranged in different combinations.

Storage

104

7

The Finishing Touch

INTRODUCTION

As I was gathering materials for this book, I came across many situations where a small change or accent could alter the character of a room, highlight a neglected corner, conceal a television set, or dramatize a collection. If you are working with a small space, such as a foyer, hall, closet, or dressing room, you can get lots more mileage from your space by building in.

Television plays a big role in our lives today, but the set should not dominate a room. This chapter will show ways of hiding it when not in use.

Although there is no chapter in this book devoted to built-in lighting, it plays a very important role in the built-in story, whether you are recessing lights in the ceiling to spotlight an isolated piece or to form light pools or patterns. Recessed light is also very dramatic in niches or behind valances or soffits. You will notice in many of the photographs used here that lighting is a vital accent and design element.

This chapter is called "The Finishing Touch" because, as you can see, that is just what these built-ins accomplish. Take a good look around your house and see what space can be utilized, what eyesores can be concealed, where built-in lighting can be added for drama—where you can add your own finishing touch!

Photograph courtesy of Stauffer Chemical Company

A finishing touch—built in primarily for design. A blank wall has been filled up with a geometric pattern of beams. The top shelves are for books and small objects. This is a good device to use on a busy wall covering or to form a three-dimensional supergraphic on a painted wall.

Opposite:

The bedroom is a simple room made effective by employing contrast. Painted beams, 2 by 4 inches, were used as a decorative touch only, to contrast with the dark "nylon velvet" walls. The bed is on a raised platform covered with carpeting.

The sketch shows how to dramatize a small working area by applying decorative beams to a dark wall. An inset of pegboard by the desk is useful for hanging drafting instruments.

The Finishing Touch

106

Designed by Virginia Frankel, A.S.I.D., Professional Affiliate, for American Enka, Inc.

Designed by Ernest Silva

Eight feet of empty wall—a small addition, and it becomes a focal point to display a collection above and nurture plants below.

A surface of translucent plastic embedded with bamboo and lighted from within by plant-growing bulbs from Duro-Lite casts a reflection up on the artwork and down on the plants. An added bonus: a section of the plastic-bamboo shelving at the right end lifts to reveal a light box for viewing photographic slides.

A small but effective addition for any wall.

The Finishing Touch

108

Designed by Penny Hallack Lehman, A.S.I.D.

These before and after photographs show that a minor change can make a major difference. A seldom-used pair of French doors has been converted to become a built-in bookcase and cabinet unit. The top shelves hold books, a hi-fi system, and art objects. The wire-covered cabinets below hold the speakers and records.

This is a simple alteration, built by the owner, but what a difference it makes in the overall appearance of the room.

The Finishing Touch

109

Designed by Stephen Chase of Arthur Elrod Associates, Inc.

Built-ins are equally effective indoors and out. This potting shed is in the corner of the terrace in a Florida condominium.

The triangular sides are sand-blasted weathered wood. They open on each side for storage. The center drawer unit is of plywood and has shelves of glass. All materials are applicable for indoor or outdoor use.

The Finishing Touch

110

American Olean Tile

If you are working with a builder, why not have him build some recessed niches for you? The one above the tub in this photograph is not only decorative but holds all the bath needs, towels, and beauty aids. The recessed light keeps the plants alive.

The Finishing Touch

Designed by Virginia Frankel, A.S.I.D., Professional Affiliate

The Finishing Touch

112

This sketch shows that, working around a simple fireplace, you can position your niches in the same fashion you would hang an art wall for all-over design impact.

Designed by Reuben de Saavedra, A.S.I.D.

A television set should be seen only when in use. How does one hide the "ugly eye"? Here the television set was recessed behind the center door of this bedroom armoire. It was placed on a pull-out swivel slide at viewing height so it could be used for in-bed viewing or swiveled to face the pair of chairs in front of the window—a versatile solution.

The Finishing Touch

113

Designed by Ernest Silva

A 4-foot Japanese-style tokonoma was built into this family room. The bottom sliding panels cover the television set and the side inner panels hold the hi-fi, speakers, and records.

The Finishing Touch

114

The feeling of spaciousness in the top half is created by a sparsity of objects and plants. It is subtly lit by recessed bulbs: Vita-Lite bulbs by Duro-Lite, for longer plant life.

Designed by Augusto Rojas

In designing your built-ins, you need not limit yourself to straight lines. The designer of this young girl's room took advantage of the width and put a desk and bookshelf at right angles to the wall with a high, round arch for decoration and built-in lighting.

The sketch of a dining area shows a full curve used as a pass-through from the dining room to the kitchen. Use the curve or arch as a finishing touch to add to your design.

The Finishing Touch

115

8

Multipurpose Rooms

INTRODUCTION

Multipurpose rooms are needed more and more today as our total living space shrinks. It is not only the increased costs of construction that are forcing us into smaller housing units, but also other costly items, such as taxes, land prices, and interest charges that continue even after you move in—all of which are an estimated two-thirds of the total cost. Because of this, there is an increasing need for careful space planning and multipurpose rooms, to get more living from less space.

An office at home can be combined with a den or guest room, or placed in a roomy foyer or kitchen. The second bedroom or guest room should be multipurpose, since it is not in use all the time. This space can double as an office, sewing room, or hobby area. When you are furnishing, keep in mind the uses of the room. If you are using part for sewing, painting, or ceramics, have a hard-surface floor, and anywhere you are using water or are apt to mess up the floor, just place area rugs over vinyl or tile to make maintenance simpler. If you are painting your built-ins, semigloss is better than flat paint for wiping off fingerprints.

In your initial planning, be aware of lighting. Don't wait until the units are in place to discover you have locked yourself into a dark corner by the desk or the reading chair. In your initial floor plan, indicate where your outlets are and work around them.

A dining room hides a portable dishwasher under a handsome buffet, or a roomy foyer can accommodate a Murphy bed. A built-out ledge behind a sleep sofa or window seat can provide additional storage for blankets and bedding. When the ceiling height allows, a loft bed or multi-level play area is a good space utilizer. With ingenuity and careful planning, you can take advantage of every inch, not only horizontally, but vertically as well.

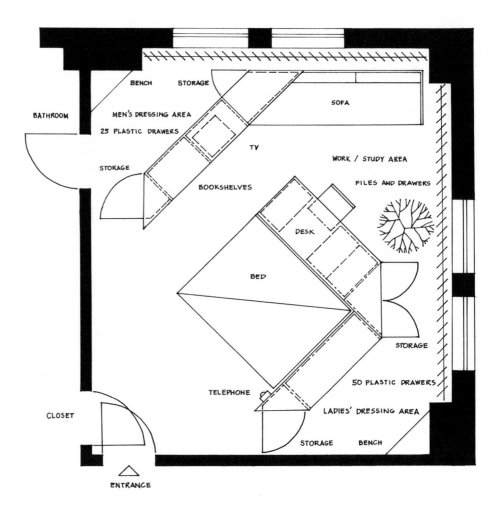

BATHROOM

BENCH   STORAGE

MEN'S DRESSING AREA

25 PLASTIC DRAWERS

STORAGE

BOOKSHELVES

SOFA

TV

WORK / STUDY AREA

FILES AND DRAWERS

DESK

BED

TELEPHONE

STORAGE

50 PLASTIC DRAWERS

LADIES' DRESSING AREA

CLOSET

STORAGE   BENCH

ENTRANCE

This combination office/sitting room/bedroom and dressing room has four freestanding plywood partitions placed carefully to keep each space functioning independently and to enable three or four people to use the room with no interference from one another.

The wall unit behind the bed holds fifty plastic drawers for the ladies dressing room; the wall is angled so each has complete privacy. The same principle was used for the men's dressing area with its recessed drawer and storage units.

The desk unit contains files and storage space, and television viewing is accessible from the bed and the sofa. The room is only 17 by 19 feet, but because of the designer's planning, it functions as a larger room, without crowding.

Multipurpose Rooms

118

Designed by Albert Herbert, A.S I.D.

Multipurpose Rooms

119

Behr International

This perfect hobby room for a film maker has a pull-down screen behind the metal cornice, ample desk and storage space for records and supplies, and the added plus of a folding bed.

These units are from Behr International. Their clean lines allow this room to double as a den or guest room and, of course, they have the advantage of being movable.

Multipurpose Rooms

120

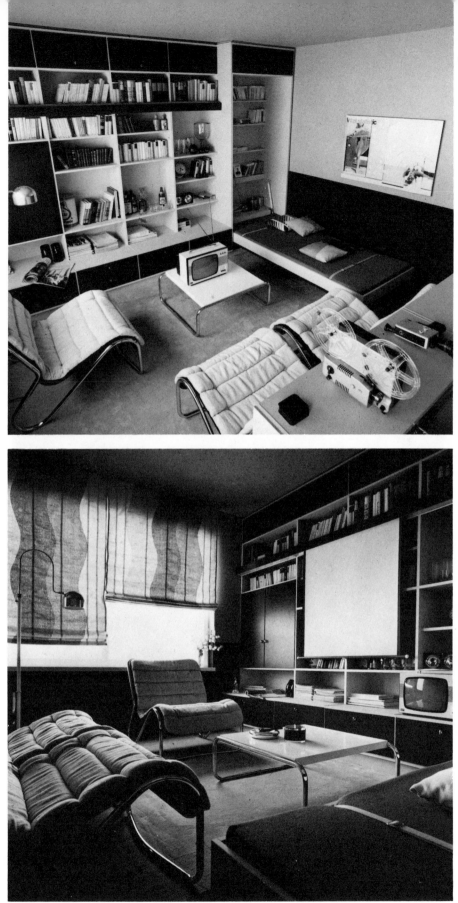

Multipurpose Rooms

Behr International

Designed by John Elmo, A.S.I.D.

An office/den designed for a man whose interests are sailing and fishing.

Built-in bookshelves, lighting, and ceiling beams add to the interest of this room. At the far end, the ceiling has been dropped to outline the desk area and form a place to hang the fishing rods. A light fascia is built over the bookshelves, and the far side of the room has built-in file drawers and storage.

Designed by Virginia Frankel, A.S.I.D., Professional Affiliate
Anso® nylon carpeting
Photograph courtesy of Allied Chemical Company

A working office at home with all the plush, luxurious feeling of a living room.

The cabinets under the recessed bookshelves hold office supplies and clutter. The bookcases and windows have been framed with a wide, flat molding repeated as a cornice to unify the room and contrast with the dark patent-leather walls.

The bottom-up laminated window shades provide not only a decorative background but also privacy and light control.

Multipurpose Rooms

123

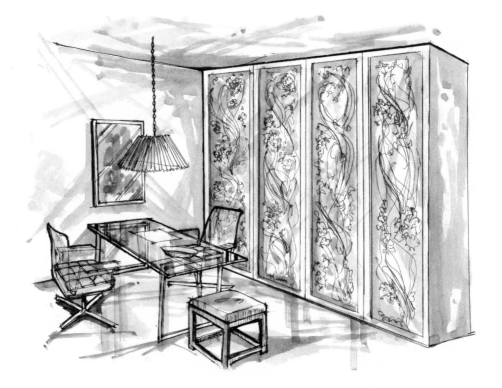

Slick, sophisticated, functional: a living room, dining room, and full office.

A steel-edge cabinet wall contains a complete office—file cabinets, record books, typewriter, and general storage. The sliding doors are fabric laminated on wood edged in metal on floor and ceiling tracks. When closed (see sketch), they form a decorative wall with fabric that matches the drapes. The desk doubles as a dining table and the U-shaped sofa offers ample seating.

This storage idea would work in many spaces—a good example of "out of sight, out of mind."

Designed by Edmund Motyka, A.S.I.D.

Designed by Harold W. Grieve, A.S.I.D.

A handsome, clean set of bunk beds; the lower one is on casters and can be pulled out to make a separate bed.

The step/night table is designed for ease in getting to the top bed. This is a new treatment for the traditional children's bed and is adaptable for guest rooms, extra attic sleeping space, or dens.

Designed by Virginia Frankel, A.S.I.D., Professional Affiliate

A freestanding bookcase and end table separate these living and dining spaces simply and pleasantly. Another built-in ledge forms the back rest for a platform with pillows to serve as a seating area.

These are the kinds of built-ins and furnishings that can be used for a budget apartment with great style.

Multipurpose Rooms

Room designed by Jerome Manashaw for Du Pont Company

A three-way parley is achieved in this dining foyer by hiding the Murphy bed behind decorative doors. The space at either side was filled in with shelves for books and art objects.

This clever idea for using space can be applied to guest rooms, one-room living, or a teen-ager's bedroom/sitting room.

Multipurpose Rooms

128

Photograph courtesy of Window Shade Manufacturers Association

The architectural framing of the window wall plus the addition of pre-fab beams gives this office/sitting room the clean look of a total built-in. The laminated window shades hide the radiator and allow light control.

The finished modular cabinets and wall-hung shelves and cabinets further the built-in illusion. A sleep sofa on the opposite wall can turn the room into a guest bedroom when necessary.

In bringing an old, lackluster room up to date, you will find that built-ins add designer touches.

Multipurpose Rooms

129

Behr International

A combination living room and office using prefab modules from Behr International. The front of these units is teak veneer.

A low divider was used to separate the living and work areas. It is deep enough to hold files, and the right-hand unit is built to the ceiling to screen the working space further. The second photograph shows the living-room side with the bar unit open.

On the office side, the space around the window has been used to provide more shelf space, and the television, when closed, matches the storage wall in the living room.

Multipurpose Rooms

130

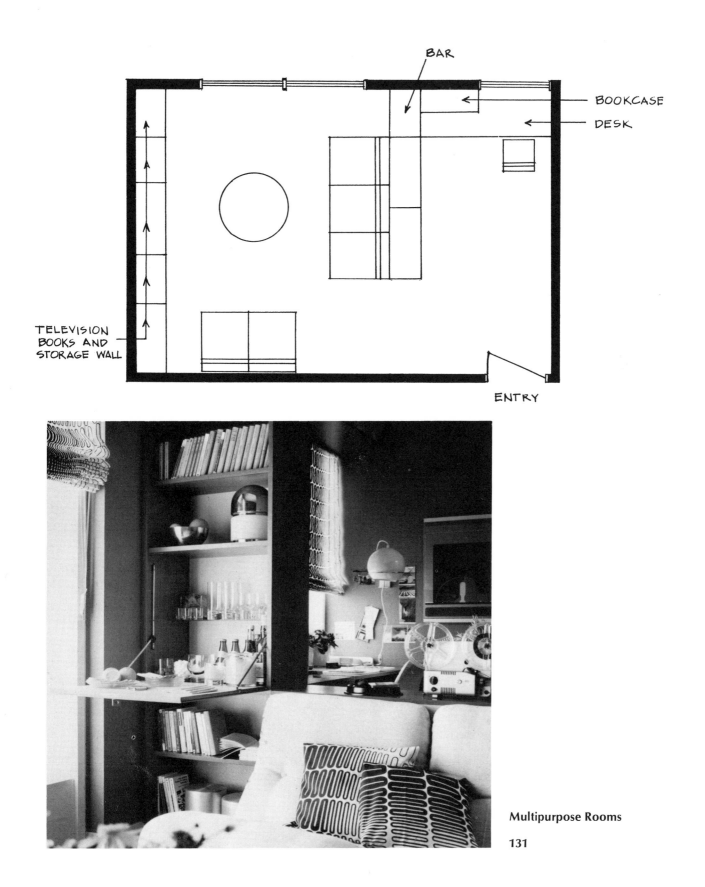

BAR

BOOKCASE

DESK

TELEVISION
BOOKS AND
STORAGE WALL

ENTRY

Multipurpose Rooms

131

9

Bedrooms and Baths

INTRODUCTION

The bedroom has come a long way from the matched sets placed around the perimeter of the room used solely for sleeping. It now also functions as a television viewing room, an extra sitting room, an office, or a hobby room. To incorporate its added functions, not only have the furnishings changed, but also their placement.

Beds are free-floating with attached storage headboards that replace the old chests of drawers. Where space allows, there are drawers in closets or built flush along a wall, also including the television set. A drop-down desk or a self-lighted dressing table on one wall frees the rest of the room. Or the same type of wall unit, but freestanding, used as a divider, isolates the bed and frees the rest of the room for daytime activities.

Depending on how many rooms you have, you can determine the priority of the bedroom design. Whether you wish to use it solely for sleeping or as a second sitting room or office provides the basis for the design.

The bathroom also has come a long way. From the once-sterile, cramped white-tiled space with chrome fixtures it has grown in size and luxury—not quite on the scale of the Roman bath, but almost. Where space allows, massage tables and saunas are included, and chaises with sunlamps overhead. Exhilarating colors are being used in towels and other bath needs created by high-fashion designers. Today's bathroom can be truly a room in which to relax and luxuriate.

The dressing room has also made a comeback, where space allows, and quite often the bedroom is divided into sleeping and dressing rooms. The old amenities are returning, and they are most welcome.

Designed by Virginia Frankel, A.S.I.D., Professional Affiliate

The floating bed is gaining popularity in today's interiors. When you place a bed in the center of the room, building in a headboard or back rest is really necessary. The built-in unit can combine any functions you wish. If lack of closet space is your problem, a contemporary version of the armoire can be built from floor to ceiling if you wish to have a hanging wardrobe. If you lack drawer space, the back rest can be built up to 5 or 6 feet to form a chest. Another use for the headboard is a desk, with storage on either side.

This bed was designed to take advantage of a corner window with a view. A floating bed on a carpeted platform with a low built-in headboard forms a giant T facing the window walls. The headboard does double duty as a storage chest and a surface for ornaments.

Floating the bed is a flexible and versatile way to arrange your bedroom.

Designed by Reuben de Saavedra, A.S.I.D.

Floating a bed in the center of a room not only is dramatic but it helps to make a small room look larger. This headboard forms a head rest and has drawers and storage space as well as end tables along the sides of the bed.

The first photograph shows the back of the bed and the second shows the end tables. One piece of furniture takes the place of four.

The unit is finished with a high-gloss lacquer for beauty and durability. The carpet covers the base of the built-in bed platform and the headboard and canopy are clear lucite.

An alcove is built on each side of the window for concealed extra closets, and a chaise is made by use of a covered mattress and pillow roll for the window seat.

Bedrooms and Baths

135

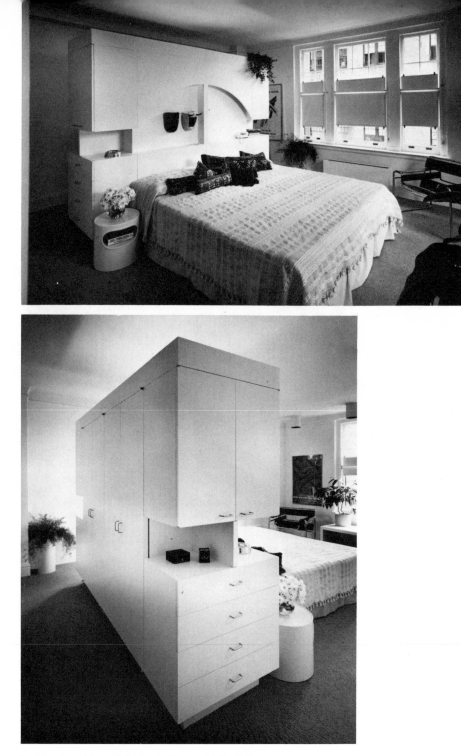

Designed by architects Robert A. M. Stern and John S. Hagmann

Another example of a free-floating bed with an architectural feeling.

The freestanding combination headboard, chest of drawers, and closet provides maximum storage. The closet area faces two existing wall closets, thus forming a dressing room.

The strong pattern and simplicity of the headboard design is all the ornamentation that the room needs.

Designed by Penny Hallack Lehman, A.S.I.D.

This charming bedroom successfully combines the old and the new. The simple lines of the built-in wall offer a pleasing contrast to the antique brass headboard, rocker, and chest of drawers. The shelves are spaced to hold an assortment of memorabilia as well as books—a good way to organize clutter.

Bedrooms and Baths

137

Designed by Stephen Chase of Arthur Elrod Associates, Inc.

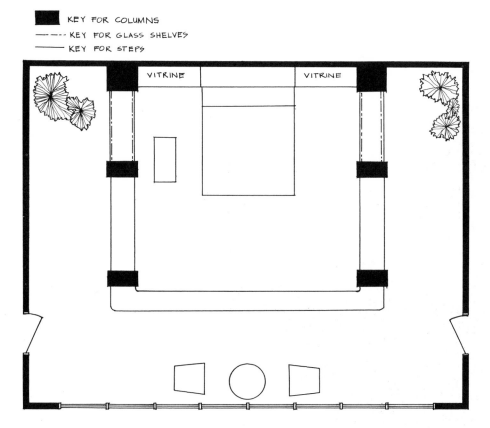

KEY FOR COLUMNS
KEY FOR GLASS SHELVES
KEY FOR STEPS

VITRINE   VITRINE

The designer has taken advantage of this spacious room in a Honolulu home to create a breathtaking bedroom. There are two steps leading up to the bed platform. The beams at each corner meet the ceiling beams with their recessed lights to create the illusion of a room within a room. Glass shelves have been placed on two sides to house a collection and the built-in cabinet next to the bed holds a wet bar.

Bedrooms and Baths

139

Photograph courtesy of I.C.F.

Bedrooms and Baths

140

A clean, simple bedroom has been designed using the Interlubke system. The hanging shelf over the bed visually replaces the headboard while serving as a bookshelf. The unit to the right of the bed is a chifforobe, and the adjoining piece opens up for a dressing table.

A contemporary look—functional, flexible, practical, and striking.

A small guest bedroom has a paneled wall, two 10-inch beams framing the bed with shelves stained to match the wall for bookcases, a small desk, and a ledge behind the bed. The bookcases are mounted on metal wall-hung brackets and the desk on angle irons. The posts are painted to match the wall.

This room can be installed on a rainy afternoon—neat but not gaudy.

Bedrooms and Baths

Designed by Stephen Chase of Arthur Elrod Associates, Inc.

A formal bedroom doubles as a working office in this Palm Springs home. The cabinet wall facing the bed has open glass shelves for a porcelain collection, and the closed cabinet over the desk holds the television set and conceals the lighting for the desk area. The pine cabinets on either side of the desk cover filing equipment and shelter other office accouterments.

As in this room, function as well as space should dictate the choice of built-ins.

Bedrooms and Baths

142

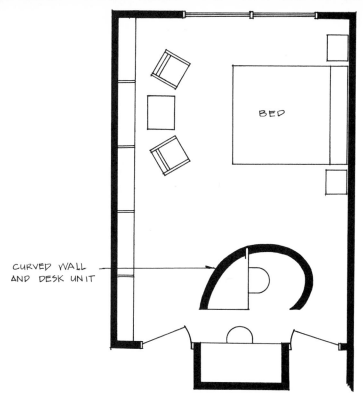

CURVED WALL
AND DESK UNIT

BED

Designed by architects Robert A. M. Stern and John S. Hagmann

A built-in, freestanding study tower encloses two small desks and isolates them from the sleeping area. By not carrying the tower to the ceiling and providing the slit for light, the size of the unit is minimized and it is kept from overpowering the room. Scale is still one of the most important components of good design.

Bedrooms and Baths

143

Designed by American Standard Co.

Bedrooms and Baths

144

In this luxurious bath the freestanding wall separates the tub from the rest of the room. Cutout niches hold towels and bath oils. The chaise is a built-in banquette under a dormer window for sunning or relaxing.

Here is everything a bath should be—aesthetically pleasing, relaxing, and comfortable.

Designed by architects Robert A. M. Stern and John S. Hagmann

A balcony bedroom makes a strong statement by the use of lighted recesses and sparse and careful placement of books and accessories in a duplex apartment. The curve of the dropped ceiling follows the flow of the balcony and is repeated in the column and recesses above the bed.

Every opportunity is used in the design of the spaces as well as of the cabinet work and furnishings to dramatize works of art of diverse sizes, and thus to vary the scale of the spaces.

Bedrooms and Baths

145

Designed by Reuben de Saavedra, A.S.I.D.

Bedrooms and Baths

146

A bedroom and dressing room with all the storage you could wish for. The dressing room has mirrored doors and drawers, each designed to hold a specific size and shape of clothes and accessories. Additional storage is found in the white formica drawer space that also holds the television set.

Designed by Virginia Frankel, A.S.I.D., Professional Affiliate

Built-in armoires create a bed/sitting room plus extra storage. The badly placed window was camouflaged with a matching door. This small room, only 11 by 14 feet, is visually enlarged by the careful construction, which is more practical than any furniture grouping could be.

Bedrooms and Baths

147

Designed by architects Robert A. M. Stern and John S. Hagmann

If you are lucky enough to have a curved wall to work with, this idea of a sink on each end instead of side by side—as is usual—and the circular sinks make a pleasing contrast to the straight-line counter.

What more could a man wish for in his own bath? Here are a barber chair and a sauna and massage table with overhead sunlamp built in.

Designed by architects Robert A. M. Stern and John S. Hagmann

Take one old bath, fill up an empty corner with a wonderful drawer and storage unit, and the entire room looks better. The units inside the shell are placed on an angle to provide maximum storage room between the drawer unit and the floor-to-ceiling shelves and door unit.

Photograph courtesy of Wallcovering Council

An old-fashioned bath updated by moving the sink out from the wall with new cabinets, a mirror, and a decorative panel at the foot of the tub.

The sink cabinet conceals the pipes and provides ample storage, leaving the open shelves free for towels and decorative accessories. The two-sided mirror is held by a dowel at the top and bottom.

A small change has made a big improvement.

Bedrooms and Baths

151

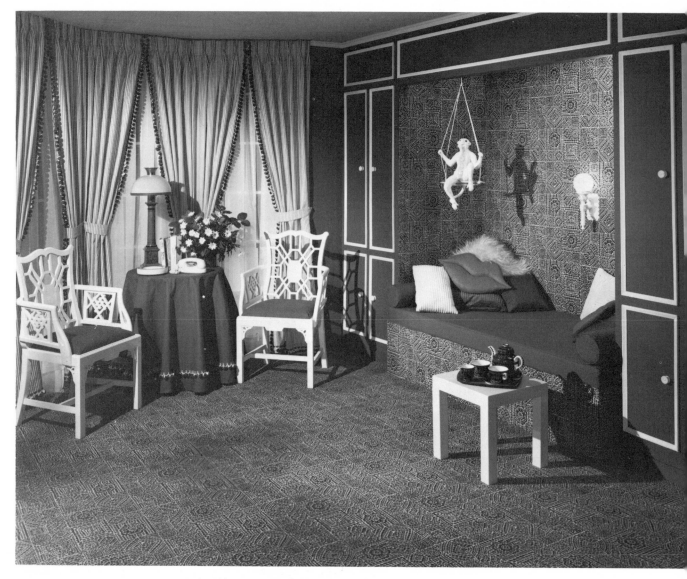

Designed by Virginia Frankel, A.S.I.D., Professional Affiliate, for Allied Chemical Company
Anso® nylon carpeting

A cheerful bedroom/sitting room. Built-in closets flank the bed and the carpet covers the bed base and lines the wall.

The built-ins are accented with applied moldings, a device that makes any cabinet work look richer.

10

Hobby Centers

INTRODUCTION

Hobby or special-interest rooms do not have to be a luxury. If you do not have the space for a separate studio or hobby room, it can be incorporated into or combined with a bedroom or den, or tucked away in the corner of an attic or basement.

Each special-interest room usually has one major requirement. After that has been met, the design of the room revolves around it. For a studio, you need good natural light. For a photographer's retreat or a horticulturist, a water source is needed. For a collector, adequate lighting, enough voltage, and display space are required. For a music room, location and soundproofing take precedence.

Next, take into account that not only enough storage but also the proper size, depth, height, and width of your units, as well as wall and floor coverings, are important. For a room where water is used, a hard-surface flooring is advisable—this also applies to children's rooms—but softened with scatter rugs. In a music room, carpeting, drapes, and even a fabric or carpeted wall will give better sound. Speakers should be on the long wall and at least 6 feet apart and a minimum of 3 feet from the floor.

For a screening room, it is wise to have a permanent pull-down screen with the projector and sound equipment built into the facing wall with sliding or hinged doors, not only to hide the equipment when not in use but also to keep it dust-free.

Whatever your interest, there can be space planned for it in your home. Your planning and decorating should reflect your interests as well as your comfort and taste.

Designed by Edmund Motyka, A.S.I.D.
Photograph courtesy of Window Shade Manufacturers Association

So many of these rooms really fit into more than one category. For instance, this well-planned handyman's center could go equally well in the chapter on multipurpose rooms or that on window treatments. This only emphasizes that good design is many-faceted.

With the window-wall cabinets closed, this room appears to be a pleasant den and guest bedroom. The colors are yellow, white, and green and the window shades, a do-it-yourself project, have a geometric design which was applied with a small roller. Masking tape was used to lay in the abstract design.

Hobby Centers

Yet, when the cabinet doors are opened, there is a dramatic change—
a complete woodworking shop is revealed. The butcher-block desk con-
verts to a worktable and the valance opens for storage. The lower parts of
each built-in are set on casters to pull out and act as horses to cut extra-
length lumber. An exhaust fan behind the large shade draws out the
fumes of spray paints and lacquers, and the green-and-white hard-surface
floor is easy to mop and care for.

Hobby Centers

155

Designed by Edmund Motyka, A.S.I.D.
Photographs courtesy of Du Pont Company
Antron® nylon carpeting

These photographs show the versatility of one built-in wall used in two different settings.

The first room was planned for a photography buff. The counter at the right is equipped with a sink, timer, trays, chemical storage, and so on. The dryer can be set on the desk and a movie screen pulled down from the window for movies or slides. The sectional sofa can be separated or moved for television viewing as well as film showings.

The same window wall has been used to create a perfect sewing and needlework center. The sink has been omitted and a sewing machine and a pull-out platform have been installed. The niches and shelves are perfect containers for fabrics and yarns, and the drawers behind the cabinets keep all the small items in order—scissors, threads, pins, and patterns.

Hobby Centers

156

Designed by William Purvis, A.S.I.D.
Photograph courtesy Masonite Corporation

Hobby Centers

158

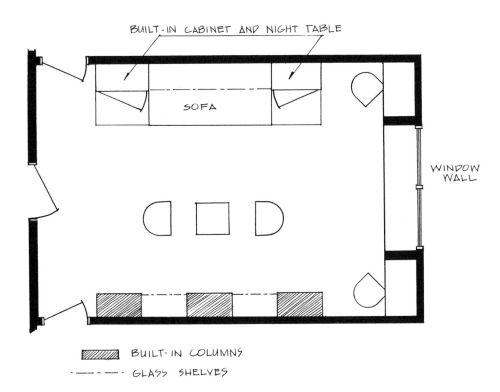

BUILT-IN CABINET AND NIGHT TABLE

SOFA

WINDOW
WALL

BUILT-IN COLUMNS

GLASS SHELVES

This attic was converted into a hobby room, a collector's showcase, and a gardening area.

Walls were paneled in Masonite and Moonspot siding painted white, and the columns were built of rosewood paneling for contrast. These columns can be placed any distance apart, with regular or irregular spacing, depending on the type of collection and the overall design desired. The corner wall-hung desk and plant shelf are covered with formica. This is a simple and pleasing room in which to relax.

Taking poetic license, I designed the wall facing the one in the photograph to hold a daybed and repeat the design of the rosewood columns. The columns have been extended 18 inches at the base to serve as end tables; a touch latch on the upper part hides shelving. The base of the bed has drawers for linens and pillows, and the frosted glass shelf, framed in wood, hides fluorescent tubes softly lighting the bed wall and the objects above.

Hobby Centers

159

Designed by architects Bull, Field, Volkmann, and Stockwell
Photograph courtesy of California Redwood Association

For a horticulturist, no room is complete without plants. These two mini greenhouses add an unusual feature to the bath.

Certainly this takes space, money, and the right setting. The luxury of two greenhouses on either side of the tub is not physically possible for everyone, but even a smaller version of this, in the conventional apartment bath, could be achieved if you have high ceilings. How about using the space over the tub and enclosing it in glass? Or just leave it open with hanging plants. Or construct a greenhouse in the window area of an unused corner.

Designed by Robert J. King, A.S.I.D., for Uniroyal, Inc.
Photograph courtesy of Uniroyal, Inc.

This mini gym shows how to convert an extra room into a health center.
The space used is only 12 by 14 feet. The exercise platform is covered
with Naugahyde. The spaces on each side of the built-in shelves are
mirrored, and the niches are used for gym equipment, exercise bars, and
a collection of old apothecary jars containing sun lotions. With the radio
and books it is not only a gym but a comfortable hideaway as well.

Hobby Centers

161

Photograph courtesy of Singer Sewing Machine Company

A lot of thought and careful planning have gone into this sewing center/den. It is completely equipped with boxes for fabrics; pegs to hold spools; shallow drawers for patterns, pins, and small objects; ample storage for the ironing board, dummy, and sewing machine; and the luxury of a large surface for laying out patterns and cutting fabric—all are there.

To convert the workshop back into a den, one needs only to fold the table flush against the shelves. The chest of drawers rolls back into the niche and the folding doors are closed. A perfect solution for a dual-purpose room.

Hobby Centers

162

Designed by Virginia Frankel, A.S.I.D., Professional Affiliate

This living room was designed to hold all the equipment needed by the winter-sports fan. It is also an attractive room for lounging.

On each side of the fireplace, seating has been built in with storage underneath—one side for ice skates, the other for log storage. On either side of these are open vertical boxes in which to keep skis. The cabinets under the trophy cases and bookshelves store mittens, hats, scarves, and other items. The snowshoes have been hung over the fireplace not only to get them out of the way but also as a decorative accent in keeping with the rest of the room.

Hobby Centers

Room design and furniture by Atelier International, Ltd.

This room is not technically a hobby center, but it is a collector's dream.

The plexiglass panels along the wall are built in on glides. The outer frame can be removed to change the lithograph or print. The mats are held in place by small lucite pegs. The runners enable the owner to change the placement of his artwork at will.

Hobby Centers

164

The carpeted steps serve a dual purpose. The bottom drawer pulls out to hold the balance of the collection, a function that could be achieved only by careful design and building in.

11

Do It Yourself

INTRODUCTION

You do not have to be an accomplished carpenter to try many of the ideas shown here. With a few good tools, lumber precut to your measurements, and a definite plan of what you want to make, you are on your way! Graph paper is very helpful in planning. If you draw your design on it, making every square (or four squares) equal to one foot, you can see your proportions and make the work easier.

When you take measurements, make sure that the dimensions—inside or outside—will allow room for your wood, whether ½ or ¾ inch thick. Also, leave a few inches of breathing space. The average depth for books is 7 to 8 inches, and for art and larger books, 12 to 14 inches. Measure your largest book and be guided by it. When designing a space for television sets or small refrigerators—in fact, any electrical appliance—leave extra room in back for air circulation. If it heats up, you may have to use a layer of asbestos for fireproofing.

Another thing to look for is molding. Whether floor, window, or ceiling, you must allow room for a cutout so your pieces fit flush against the wall. For cabinets and bookcases, allow for a baseboard. If you are building a large piece, a recessed base will keep it from looking heavy.

Also, be aware of where your electrical outlets are. Keep appliances near outlets and do not mistakenly block any that you need.

TAKING MEASUREMENTS

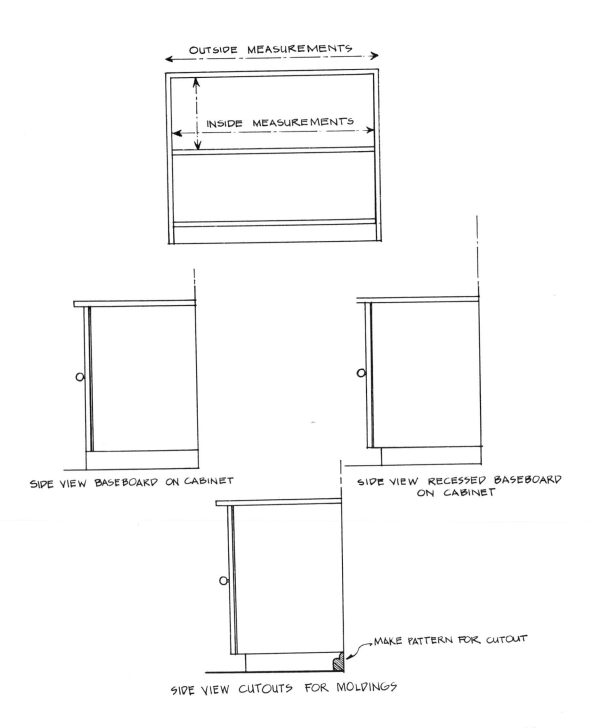

OUTSIDE MEASUREMENTS

INSIDE MEASUREMENTS

SIDE VIEW BASEBOARD ON CABINET

SIDE VIEW RECESSED BASEBOARD ON CABINET

MAKE PATTERN FOR CUTOUT

SIDE VIEW CUTOUTS FOR MOLDINGS

Do It Yourself

166

The sketch shows how to measure some of the things mentioned here. By mixing accurate measurements with a dash of imagination and a colorful finish, a new hobby is born.

Designed by Edmund Motyka, A.S.I.D.
G.A.F. flooring

A much-used and much-abused "mudroom" and main entrance to a home in Maine was organized with a very simple but practical storage system. A raised platform was built to hold logs and for easy seating to remove boots and rubbers. Each member of the family has his or her own section for coats, hats, mittens, and so forth. Paint cans sprayed in vivid colors were piled up for skates and boot storage—a very effective and inexpensive storage idea.

Hard-surface flooring was laid to make this room practical and handsome. The white-brick pattern contrasts stunningly with the vivid colors of the walls, paint cans, and multicolored blinds.

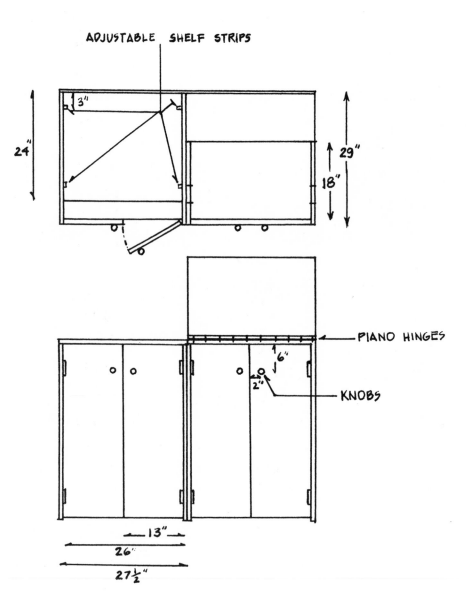

ADJUSTABLE SHELF STRIPS

3"

24"

29"

18"

PIANO HINGES

KNOBS

6"

2"

13"

26"

27½"

This ingenious design could fit into many categories. It not only moves with you but rolls from room to room.

It was planned to house a convertible dishwasher. There was not enough room in the kitchen of this house to install a permanent dishwasher, so this unit was designed as a buffet in the dining room. After the dishes are loaded the dishwasher is wheeled into the kitchen, plugged in, and attached to the sink.

Designed by the Maytag Company
Photographs courtesy of the Maytag Company

The side opposite the dishwasher has adjustable shelves for storage. The tops of both sides are covered with formica and the top of the dishwasher side lifts up to enable you to see the cutting-block top of the dishwasher.

This unit has been covered with grass cloth, but paint, wallpaper, or fabric would do, depending on your decor. You could also apply moldings.

If in a future move you wished to install the dishwasher in your kitchen, the cabinet, with the addition of more shelves or a small refrigerator, could become a bar unit.

Do It Yourself

169

A small room fitted with built-in platforms and ledges could be a simple, inexpensive way to make use of an extra room. The window wall can be filled out with bookshelves. This is an easy project for the home handyman.

The ceiling studs can be covered easily and inexpensively with bamboo window blinds nailed to each wall. Canvas-covered foam mattresses cover each platform and can be used for sleeping or lounging.

Designed by Virginia Frankel, A.S.I.D., Professional Affiliate

Designed by Virginia Frankel, A.S.I.D., Professional Affiliate

The do-it-yourselfer can make a small bedroom appear larger and more dramatic with built-in four-poster beds. The posts and the outline of the top are made of 3-by-3-inch lumber nailed together and to the ceiling.

The posts are covered with the same vinyl as the floor, but they could also be treated with fabric or wallpaper, or just painted to achieve any decorative effect you choose.

Do It Yourself

172

Accurate measurements and careful planning can increase your storage space. You will discover that by dividing space this way and building in partitions, shelves, drawers, or whatever, you will get more use from the space.

This closet was designed around the measurements of the hat boxes, dress bags, blanket bags, and plastic boxes generally found in stores. One section on the right was filled with cardboard files and covered with the same vinyl used in the closet accessories. When planning the divisions, measure the hat boxes and determine how much linear space you need for them. Count the number of shoes and measure the depth and running feet needed to hold them. Plan this way so that no space is wasted. This also applies to your kitchen, books, records, and office storage. Sometimes you may have to live in your home for a while before your storage needs are apparent; it is worth waiting.

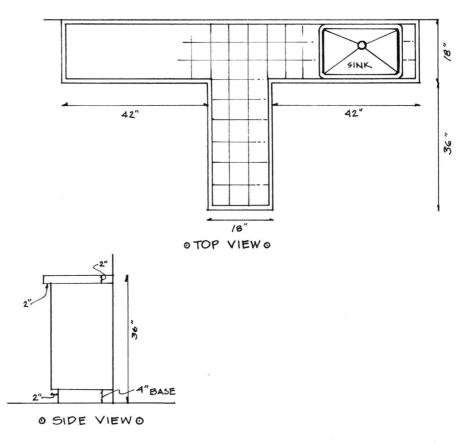

VINYL TILE ON COUNTER TOP

18"

36"

42"   42"

18"

◦ TOP VIEW ◦

2"

2"

36"

2"   4" BASE

◦ SIDE VIEW ◦

SINK

Do It Yourself

174

A built-in counter, cabinet, sink cover, and gardening storage space serves as both a decorative and a practical divider. The cabinets facing the breakfast table hold the china and linen, and the tops of the units are covered with the same hard-surface vinyl as the floor, to take the abuse of the potting center and sink.

Designed by Virginia Frankel, A.S.I.D., Professional Affiliate

Do It Yourself

It is a room divider, a storage wall, or with a back added to the top section, a freestanding wall.

This movable divider made of Masonite and caster-mounted has multiple uses—to create a foyer, to isolate a dining area, to provide a work space, or as in the second photo, to form a hobby center.

The model-train table folds into the paneled wall when not in use. The table legs can be painted or furnished with decorative fabric to give added interest to the rear wall. I have made two floor plans to show you additional uses of this unit.

In plan 1 I have used three 8-foot Masonite movable dividers to partition a one-room apartment, forming a U in the middle of the room that isolates the dining area and provides storage for dishes and table linens. The sleep sofa backs up to one of them in the living area and a chest along one wall holds clothing and accessories.

Plan 2 is a similar room but the dividers are in 6-foot lengths, again for one-room living, but creating a foyer as well as a dining room to show the unlimited possibilities that this type of unit can have. To make it even more versatile, the units, whether in 6-foot or 8-foot sections, can be divided in half and built in 3- and 4-foot sections.

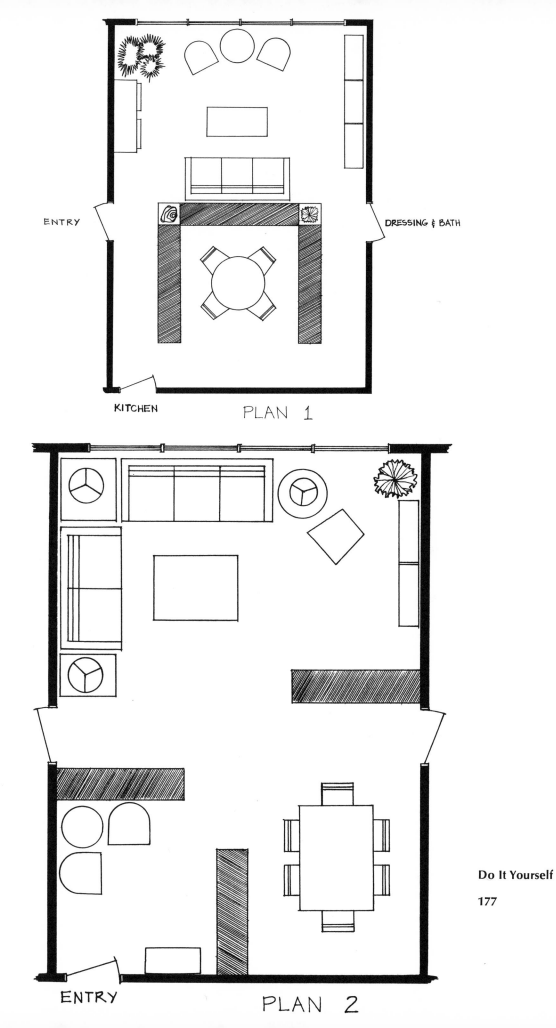

ENTRY

DRESSING & BATH

KITCHEN

PLAN 1

ENTRY

PLAN 2

Do It Yourself

177

Designed by Virginia Frankel,
A.S.I.D., Professional Affiliate

Designed by Edmund Motyka, A.S.I.D.

What an ingenious and versatile idea! The lumberyard cut a series of 18-inch square pine boards; these were nailed together, covered with wallpaper, stacked—and voilà, instant built-ins!

With the same idea I have designed a totem pole, with one addition—the wing and top boxes have five sides so they can be nailed to the wall for extra support.

It is fun to work with these. You can, of course, use any size box and any finish you desire. The combinations and designs are unlimited.

Do It Yourself

178

Photograph courtesy of Duro-Lite Corporation

An "at-home" office tucked away in a closet. The ceiling of decorative plastic hides the fluorescent lighting by Duro-Lite and casts an even light on the desk surface.

The back pegboard wall is handy for shelf strips and hanging pictures and the desk top rests on a pair of two-drawer file cabinets. Try this for your first installation. All you need are nails to hang the pegboard, ready-made doors to install, and a pail of paint, and you will be hooked.

Do It Yourself

179

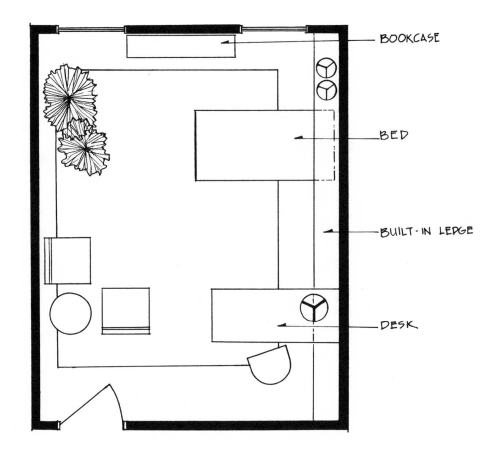

BOOKCASE

BED

BUILT-IN LEDGE

DESK

By using simple children's wooden stools, an unusual and handsome bookcase has been put together. Stained pine planks form the shelves; no fastening is necessary. A matching pine plank running the length of the room functions as a night table and ledge for decorative accessories. Both the ledge and the desk are fastened to the wall with angle irons and finished with a coat of wax. The metal legs of the desk can be bought in any hardware store and the frame that holds the mattress is also easy to construct.

Inexpensive chairs and light fixtures make this well within reach of anybody's budget.

Do It Yourself

180

Designed by Edmund Motyka, A.S.I.D.

Do It Yourself

181

Photographs courtesy of the Maytag Company

Two small touches to simplify your kitchen storage. The silverware holder is the same idea you have seen many times in a cafeteria—separate containers for each utensil set in a pull-out shelf for easy access. The top shelf holds flat dividers for larger utensils.

Removing one of your cabinet doors, giving it a new base on glides and a pegboard side, makes your pots and pans visually appealing and eliminates the need to pull them all out to reach the bottom one on the pile.

Another version of this would be having the pegboard panel in the center of the door for hanging storage on both sides.

12

Attics and Basements

INTRODUCTION

No longer a catchall for old trouble, about-to-be-discarded furniture and cartons, or designed in "Early Salvation Army," the attic has had a facelift and with proper insulation can be rejuvenated into a child's room, guest room, hobby room, or efficiently organized storage room.

When designing an attic, take advantage of any irregular spaces under dormer window or eaves. These spaces work for storage, tables, desks, or built-in seating.

The basement with boiler, wood pile, and pipes carefully concealed, and all signs of "Early Trash" hidden, has been converted into a den, an office, a second sitting room, laundry center, or workshop and hobby room. Ceiling pipes can be masked with a coat of paint and small windows dressed up to appear larger.

In the basement, take special care with your lighting so you do not feel you are in a cave. If you have high, small windows or no windows, design a window frame or lambrequin. Set it 6 to 8 inches from the window frame and have a light tube behind, either fluorescent or lumiline. The light shining behind a casement, shoji, or whatever you choose will give the illusion of daylight. Another way to illuminate is with a dropped ceiling. For this you need at least a 10-foot ceiling. This is not a job for an amateur but you can get components that will fit the space and have your handyman or electrician install them for you.

Both the attic and the basement function well as a child's playroom. Whatever you use them for, from top to bottom, you have made your space work for you.

Designed by Edmund Motyka, A.S.I.D.
Photograph courtesy of G.A.F. Corp.

Attics and Basements

184

Attics are natural for construction with all their angles and nooks. There is a great deal of wasted space to which most conventional furniture will not adapt.

This attic room is one of the best examples I have seen. The space under the eaves has been used for a desk, built-in bed, sewing center, book storage, and window seat. Shelves surrounding the windows and recessed in the end of the desk are cardboard file boxes covered with colorful vinyl that picks up the colors in the hard-surface floor. A perfect way to get the most mileage for your space.

Designed by Virginia Frankel, A.S.I.D., Professional Affiliate

If you are lucky enough to have ceiling windows in your attic eaves, utilize the wall space underneath to take advantage of the light.

This built-in workbench with room for three to work, side by side, is a simple and inexpensive use of this space.

Designed by Augusto Rojas

There are so many ways to make a bedroom individual. It should be restful and pleasant to retire to, a room you can enjoy during the daytime.

This attic room takes advantage of the ceiling beams. The headboard is two straight boards cut the same width as the beams and fastened on the wall to look as though they join. Then all the beams and uprights and the ceiling are painted the same color for effect. The built-in night tables also line up with the beams.

A minimum of building for a maximum of charm.

Use the eaves of an attic to design an extra bedroom. By building a bed on each side of a dormer window with a built-in canopy effect you can make this room as dressy or as informal as you wish.

Designed and photographed by the Maytag Company

An all-purpose work center in your basement. One side is a compact laundry area with a washer, dryer, hamper, and plenty of locked cabinets for laundry supplies and drawers for children's toys and games.

Clear plexiglass separates the two units in the center and prevents sawdust from falling on the laundry side. Under-counter lights are used on both sides and the pipes for the laundry equipment are masked in the area between the unit frame and the cement block wall.

The mini shop on the other side of the cube has a workbench with open and closed storage for tools and equipment. The backs of the cabinets are lined with pegboard to hold small tools and organize clutter.

This is a solution that makes doing laundry or repairs a pleasure.

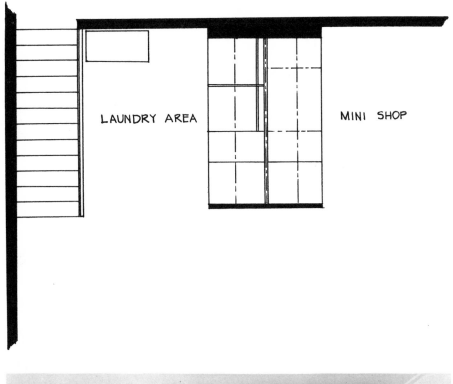

LAUNDRY AREA   MINI SHOP

Attics and Basements

189

Designed by Virginia Frankel, A.S.I.D., Professional Affiliate
Anso® carpeting by Allied Chemical Company

My basement was never like this!

Carpeted levels have been built for seating and a conversation pit created to hold the overflow. Shoji panels carry out the Oriental theme and hide fluorescent tubing to simulate the feeling of windows and cast a pleasant, subdued light throughout.

Photographs courtesy of the Maytag Company

Any chore is easier when you are well organized. This basement wall shows what can be done in a small space.

The roll-out bin to the right of the washer and dryer can be moved to the bottom of the steps or anywhere to collect the laundry. The colored drawers for sorting have holes, side and bottom, for ventilation. The top cabinet holds detergents and laundry products. Finished wash gets put into labeled boxes for family pickup and the small built-in ledge to the right holds a sewing machine and mending equipment. A built-in fluorescent light box gives adequate light for the entire work area.

Attics and Basements

191

Designed by Virginia Frankel, A.S.I.D., Professional Affiliate
Anso® nylon carpeting

Every inch of wall space has been used to turn this basement into a family room with space planned for multiple activities.

The long wall has a formica-covered cabinet to take abuse as a serving counter or bar. A portable refrigerator is hidden behind the cabinets, which provide ample storage for dishes and snacks. The top shelf holds books and speakers and under the valance a screen rolls down to show home movies. The stair wall has a built-in desk and shelves for the record player, record albums, and so on. The cube in the foreground has a hinged back to store the projector. The cube and the seating units are on casters to add to the mobility of the room.

Attics and Basements

192

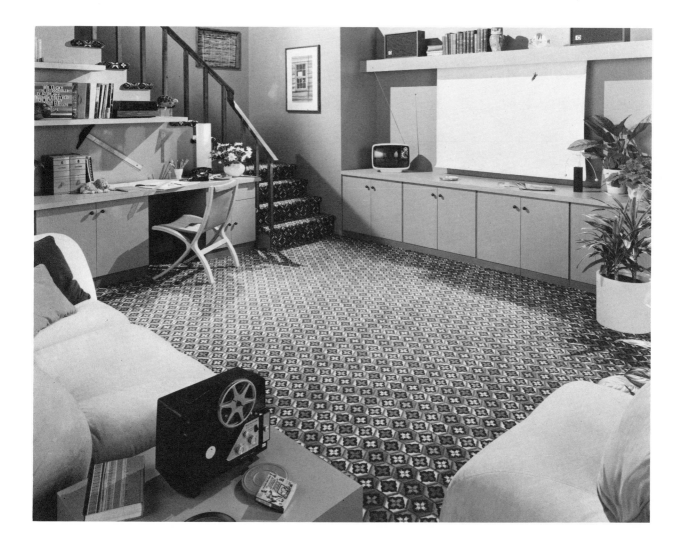

Attics and Basements

Designed by Edmund Motyka, A.S.I.D.

White and lots of green, and the use of built-ins, have transformed a dark basement into a charming second sitting room. A built-in banquette can also be used as a guest bed, flanked by bookshelves on either side.

By using a dropped ceiling with built-in lighting and a hard-surface flooring to reflect the light, a dark, windowless space is made functional and attractive.

CREDITS

Courtesy of Allied Chemical, pages 16, 47, 123, 152, 190, 192, 193

Courtesy of American Enka, Inc., pages 39, 61, 65, 107

Courtesy of American Standard Co., pages 111, 144

Atelier International, Ltd., 595 Madison Avenue, New York, N.Y. 10022—Room and Furniture Design, page 164

Banks, Richard, Architect, pages 10, 11, 36, 37

Behr International, Furniture Design and Manufacturer; Distributor: Lacour-Denno, 964 Third Avenue, New York, N.Y. 10022, pages 22, 23, 29, 49, 68, 69, 82, 83, 120, 121, 130, 131

Beylerian, Ltd., 315 East 63rd Street, New York, N.Y. 10022, page 84

Bull, Field, Volkmann and Stockwell, Architects, page 60

Cado Systems, 979 Third Avenue, New York, N.Y. 10022, pages 73, 74

Courtesy of California Redwood Association, pages 15, 30, 160

Chase, Stephen, Designer, Arthur Elrod Associates, Inc., pages 18, 66, 110, 138, 142

Courtesy of Collins & Aikman, page 141

Darar, Abby, Designer, page 38

De Saavedra, Reuben, A.S.I.D., Designer, pages 13, 55, 56, 78, 113, 135, 146

Courtesy of Du Pont Company, pages 6, 128, 156, 157

Courtesy of Duro-Lite Lamps, Inc., pages 108, 114, 179

Courtesy of Eastman Kodak, page 9

Elmo, John, F.A.S.I.D., Designer, pages 73, 122

El-Zoghby, Gamal, Architect, pages 4, 5

Frankel, Virginia, A.S.I.D., Professional Affiliate, Designer, pages 8, 9, 16, 27, 32, 33, 39, 40, 46, 47, 52, 54, 57, 59, 60, 61, 62, 67, 77, 81, 85, 86, 87, 90, 91, 94, 95, 96, 98, 99, 100, 101, 102, 103, 104, 107, 112, 123, 127, 134, 147, 152, 163, 171, 172, 175, 186, 190, 192, 193

Fuchs, Carl, Designer, page 24

Courtesy of G.A.F. Corp., pages 38, 167, 172, 175, 184, 185

Grieve, Harold W., A.S.I.D., Designer, page 126

Hagmann, John S., Architect, pages 7, 14, 19, 41, 44, 45, 48, 80, 88, 136, 143, 145, 148, 150

Herbert, Albert, A.S.I.D., Designer, pages 26, 118, 119

Interlubke System, Distributor: I.C.F., 145 East 57th Street, New York, N.Y. 10022, pages 25, 31, 34, 140

Jeffrey, Noel, Designer, page 71

King, Robert J., A.S.I.D., Designer, page 161

Kirsch, William Weber, Architect, page 15

Kosovitz, Herbert, Architect, page 3

Lehman, Penny Hallack, A.S.I.D., Designer, pages 109, 137

Malino, Emily, A.S.I.D., Designer, page 53

Manashaw, Jerome, Designer, page 128

Courtesy of Masonite Corporation, pages 158, 176

Courtesy of the Maytag Company, pages 89, 168, 169, 182, 188, 189, 191

Motyka, Edmund, A.S.I.D., Designer, pages 74, 75, 124, 125, 154, 156, 157, 167, 178, 181, 184, 194

Purvis, William L., A.S.I.D., Designer, page 158

Ranalli, George, Architect, page 17

Rojas, Augusto, Designer, pages 72, 115, 187

Courtesy of Singer Sewing Machine Company, page 162

Silva, Ernest, Designer, pages 108, 114

Courtesy of Stauffer Chemical Company, page 106

Stern, Robert A. M., Architect, pages 7, 14, 19, 41, 44, 45, 48, 80, 88, 136, 143, 145, 148, 150

Thibault, François E., A.S.I.D., Designer, pages 42, 43

Courtesy of Uniroyal, Inc., pages 149, 161

Courtesy of U.S. Plywood/Champion International, pages 36, 37, 57, 67, 77

Courtesy of Wallcovering Council, page 151

Courtesy of Window Shade Manufacturers Association, pages 24, 53, 54, 62, 92, 93, 129, 154, 155

Credits